OLDER ADULTS AND AUTISM SPECTRUM CONDITIONS

by the same author

Understanding and Working with the Spectrum of Autism
An Insider's View
ISBN 978 1 85302 971 4
eISBN 978 1 84642 229 4

Life Behind Glass
A Personal Account of Autism Spectrum Disorder
ISBN 978 1 85302 911 0
eISBN 978 0 85700 371 3

The Passionate Mind
How People with Autism Learn
ISBN 978 1 84905 121 7
eISBN 978 0 85700 313 3

Concepts of Normality
The Autistic and Typical Spectrum
ISBN 978 1 84310 604 3
eISBN 978 1 84642 829 6

Friendships
The Aspie Way
ISBN 978 1 84310 427 8
eISBN 978 1 84642 524 0

OLDER ADULTS AND AUTSM SPECTRUM CONDITIONS

AN INTRODUCTION AND GUIDE

Wenn Lawson

Foreword by Carol Povey

Jessica Kingsley *Publishers*
London and Philadelphia

First published in 2015
by Jessica Kingsley Publishers
73 Collier Street
London N1 9BE, UK
and
400 Market Street, Suite 400
Philadelphia, PA 19106, USA

www.jkp.com

Library of Congress Cataloging in Publication Data
Lawson, Wenn, 1952- , author.
  Older adults and autism spectrum conditions : an introduction and guide / Wenn Lawson ;
foreword by
Carol Povey.
     p. ; cm.
  Includes bibliographical references and index.
  ISBN 978-1-84905-961-9 (alk. paper)
  I. Title.
  [DNLM: 1. Child Development Disorders, Pervasive--physiopathology. 2. Child
Development Disorders,
Pervasive--psychology. 3. Aged. 4. Health Services for the Aged. WM 203.5]
  RC553.A88
  616.85'882--dc23
                                    2015006245

British Library Cataloguing in Publication Data
A CIP catalogue record for this book is available from the British Library

ISBN 978 1 84905 961 9
eISBN 978 0 85700 813 8

Printed and bound in Great Britain

For the past 30 years, my partner and soulmate has walked beside me. She never lags behind or marches quickly ahead. We don't always agree or appreciate the same things, but our values and commitment to each other's wellbeing never waver. Others may not see her as she stands in the background but I know she is there. She doesn't like the limelight or lots of fuss – she leaves that to me. But without her support and encouragement, I'd feel less sure of myself and of the world we both share.

This book is dedicated to my partner, as well as those other unseen heroes who make getting older in a changing world less frightening. We need you. Thanks for holding our hands, for telling us it will be OK and for being who you are. Without you, we mightn't make it.

Taking the road well-travelled

So, come with me and let us see,
Just what the issues are.
For young and old,
Heads of hair or bald,
Wrinkled, whiskered, dimpled and old,
We walk together into the far.

The far-away that's creeping closer,
The land of unknown and outgrown,
The time when sleep takes over
And the prime of our time is past.
For you and for me without any exceptions,
The ghost of ourselves with mirror reflections,
Of all that we used to be.

I used to have familiarity,
I used to know what to expect.
But now life is so confusing
I remember everything.
What must I do to forget?

Wenn Lawson

CONTENTS

Foreword

Across my professional lifetime, I have had the privilege of growing older alongside many people on the autism spectrum. I have seen awareness of autism grow, whilst being acutely aware of the many struggles individuals and families have had to encounter due to a lack of understanding and inadequate support.

In the early part of my career, whilst working with young adults, almost all the literature on autism described children. They were written either by researchers or by parents, or in some case, both, such as the exceptionally wise and insightful Dr Lorna Wing. By the very nature of these books being written from an outsider's point of view, they largely described behaviours, rather than feelings, motivations and experiences. This stated to change in the 1980s. First, adults on the spectrum started writing about their own lives, telling us how they saw and were experiencing the world, and then there started to be a recognition that autistic children grew up to be autistic adults. The same is now happening with regard to the fact that autistic adults are moving into middle and older age, telling us how that feels and what would help to make it easier.

Many challenges and joys of growing older are universal, but there are some issues which are specific to autism, and may be experienced differently to the typical population. The transition which takes place when parents, partners and contemporaries pass away, the transition following retirement and the physical transition from sprightly health towards frailty all pose different challenges to people on the autism spectrum. Yet as people are going through these transitions and may need tailored services, understanding and support to successfully steer their way through, they are likely to experience poorer services and less understanding of the condition. For many people, the image of autism that comes to mind is likely to be a young boy, either conforming to the stereotype of a little professor or a rocking, severely disabled child within a stressed, exhausted family. But autism is heterogeneous; everyone with autism is a unique human being, with their own personality, history, talents and struggles. Few people would picture a retired, older woman when thinking of autism, yet she may need just as specialist support and understanding as do the young family soon after diagnosis.

Many people on the autism spectrum who have lived independently, adapting their environment, will struggle if, due to increasing care needs, they have to accept carers into their home, or move into a group environment. Staff working in care homes for older people may never knowingly have come across autism in older adults, therefore practical strategies about how to care for someone appropriately, and how to ensure they are involved in their own care and decision makings, are vital.

We all need a sense of control in our own lives. Yet for older people with autism, there need to be conscious actions to make sure it happens. Whilst treating people with care and dignity is an essential starting point, it is not enough. Without some knowledge and understanding of autism, actions borne out of kindly intentions could be a nightmare for people on the autism spectrum.

Sadly, many of the people I know on the autism spectrum have had reason to mistrust the system. They may have had bad experiences in their lives with professionals who struggle to understand and respond to their needs, or perhaps even disbelieve them. This can have a serious impact in older age when everyone needs more healthcare to stay fit and well. An awareness of autism in older adults should therefore be a part of every healthcare professionals' toolkit.

There is still so much we don't know. In this book, Wenn explores aspects of growing older with autism, bringing to life not only his own experience, but the lived experience of many people on the autism spectrum. These examples demonstrate some of the challenges faced by people with autism, but also the many, creative ways they, and others, have found to minimise the difficulties of growing older with autism. This book is a way of sharing these practical strategies, and of helping people to think through how they can support older people, their families, friends and carers, to maximise opportunities to live the life they choose.

We are at the beginning of a journey of understanding, and this book is a worthy companion as we move forward together.

Carol Povey
Director of the Centre for Autism
National Autistic Society

ACKNOWLEDGEMENTS

It's not easy acknowledging we are no longer as young as we once were. I am reminded of the song 'Keep young and beautiful, if you want to be loved…' I acknowledge that ageing is a process and an honour; one I'm fortunate to be travelling through. Youth has its place and is very special, but it's only a prelude to being older.

Thanks to Jessica Kingsley Publishers for your patience, persistence and commitment to seeing this book through to its final stages. It's been quite a journey and one that you have walked with me, despite the obstacles.

Thanks to Ann – I wouldn't have gotten here without your editorial support and encouragement.

Thanks to my fellow autistic adults who completed those questionnaires and shared your stories with me. Without your commitment to letting the world know your view, we wouldn't have this book.

PREFACE

This book is a practical guide for professionals and carers that uses current research to highlight appropriate interventions and support for older individuals living with autism spectrum conditions (ASC).

While drawing from the larger body of general research around ASC as it affects the ageing ASC population, this book particularly includes information about research into five key areas for ASC ageing individuals compared with both children with ASC and neurotypical (NT) older individuals. These five differences relate to memory, movement, sensory profiling, language and autonomy.

The book is designed to give insight into the needs and appropriate care of older people with ASC. Each chapter covers an important aspect of everyday life, including such issues as change, personality responses, communications and stress support needs. Wherever appropriate, real-life stories are included to support and illustrate the data.

This practical research-based guide will, I hope, provide the information needed so that both professionals and carers and, indeed, individuals with ASC themselves, can increase their understanding of the condition and thus take steps to improve the lives of older individuals with autism.

Definition of Autism Spectrum Conditions (ASC) and Ageing

Ageing and autism

Ageing with autism spectrum conditions (ASC) shares some similarities to ageing without ASC, but it is also very different because the ASC brain is functionally different from that in neurotypical (NT) development.

Ageing implies a progressive deterioration of physiological function, an intrinsic age-related process of loss of vitality and an increase in vulnerability. This process is also known as senescence. However, in humans, and many other animals, the converse of senescence is the accumulated years of knowledge and wisdom that one hopes will be useful to younger generations.

Perhaps because youth is so highly valued, we often fail to see the usefulness of being an older person. Unfortunately, our main associations with ageing are more connected to disability, disease and death, and these aspects of being human impact us all. Trying to hold on to youth, or simply not preparing for the process of ageing, doesn't make ageing less likely. Rather, so much as it may hinder us in building a future that best supports us. A better option is to prepare for this period of our lives with appropriate attention.

The purpose of this book is to identify ageing issues specific to (or more pronounced in) ageing individuals with ASC compared with individuals without ASC. This applies to ASC individuals post-retirement age. The explanations, personal perspectives and tips for coping with change should help professionals and families caring for older people with ASC. The book will also be useful for those of us living and ageing with ASC.

The number of people diagnosed with ASC is increasing. Whether this is due to professionals getting better at recognising and diagnosing the condition (especially in females and in high-functioning individuals) or, as some suggest (e.g. Casanova *et al.* 2013), due to environmental change is unclear. What is clear is that the increased incidence of ASC, combined with the general increase in the ageing population, means that an ASC tidal wave is washing towards the aged-care sector. This book will help prepare the sector to meet the needs of ageing autistic adults whether home-based or in residential care.

What does ASC look like?

Autism spectrum conditions (ASC), according to the *DSM-5* (American Psychiatric Association 2013), are assessed using two criteria:

- difficulties with the social and communication domain
- difficulties due to a restricted repetitive interest and behaviour domain.

The latter category could also be considered as being 'extremely single-minded' and/or having 'deeply focused attention' (Belmonte 2000; Dern 2008; Harmon 2010; Lawson 1998/2000, 2011; Murray 1992; Murray, Lesser and Lawson 2005). These two criteria replace the previous diagnostic criteria known as the 'triad of impairments' (American Psychiatric Association 2000). The triad was made up of difficulties with social understanding, communication and social imagination.

To qualify for a diagnosis of ASC, difficulties must exist in both *DSM-5* domains. There may also be sensory dysphoria (problems), either hyper (over-sensitive) or hypo (under-sensitive), causing a person to over- or under-react to their environment. However, such characteristics outlined in *DSM-5* may not manifest until the environmental demands outweigh the ability to cope. Social expectations in today's society, from working lunches to parents being asked to get involved in school fundraising, are higher than ever, and this may be one reason why more 'older adults' are being diagnosed with ASC than ever before. Of course, other reasons are simply better diagnostic tools, more awareness and less stigma.

Other issues accompanying the above criteria are known as specifiers. Specifiers may be peculiar to the individual (e.g. an intellectual impairment or accompanying language impairment). There may also be additional difficulties with coordination, a specific learning disability (e.g. dyscalculia or dyslexia), issues based on visual or hearing delays or differences,[1] and/or auditory processing disorder (Boddaert *et al.* 2003; Dillon *et al.* 2012; Lawson 1998/2000, 2011).

---

1   For example, Irlen Syndrome; see www.irlen.com.

All of the above come packaged in an individual with their unique personality and circumstances. ASC is not an issue where one size fits all, so every aged person with ASC needs individual support. Having said this, though, there will be certain traits and issues that apply to all older people with a diagnosis of ASC. It is these traits in common that guide the writing of this book.

Incidence of ASC

In the United Kingdom, where the population in 2011 was 63.2 million, around 700,000 individuals were living with ASC (e.g. Brugha *et al.* 2009, 2012). In the United States of America, with a population of more than 316 million in July 2013,[2] more than 3.4 million were living with ASC. Of the more than 23 million people living in Australia in June 2014 it was estimated that over 60,000 Australians over the age of 55 are living with ASC (Australian Bureau of Statistics 2014). According to data from the UK National Autistic Society (NAS), 'around 70% of people with an autism spectrum condition over 55 years of age may have only been diagnosed in the last ten years' (NAS 2013).

Clearly a significant number of our older population are living with ASC. But still many older people remain undiagnosed due to being given alternative names for conditions they live with (e.g. borderline personality disorder; schizophrenia; obsessive compulsive disorder; eating disorder; learning difficulty) (Lawson 2000). It is sometimes difficult to clarify the conditions humans live with, especially if diagnosis was made during their younger years and by

---

2   www.census.gov/popclock.

professionals who may not have had a trained eye for ASC – it is really only since the late 1990s that knowledge of ASC has become part of the training for most professionals. Of course, a second opinion can be sought if an adult or family member suspects that ASC is likely to be the reason for the difficulties a person lives with.

The UK National Autistic Society estimates that at least 1 in 100 children will be diagnosed with ASC every year. In the decades to come these children will become older people living with ASC. Developing good practice now will set up strong, flexible and person-centred standards for the future.

In addition, people who were brought up 40, 50 or 60 years ago, and would meet the requirements for an ASC diagnosis if being assessed today, remain undiagnosed. These people are now part of the ageing population (ASPECT 2015). They have gone through life without specific help or intervention, and are now elderly or ageing, still with undiagnosed ASC.

Differences between adults with ASC and ASC children

It should be emphasised that the difficulties experienced by older adults with ASC are not always the same as those experienced by children with ASC. These differences are due both to changes in brain plasticity and also to the life experiences and bodily changes of the older person with ASC. Current research suggests that adults with ASC:

- are more likely than children with ASC to read facial expressions
- are less likely to have memory issues due to increases in brain plasticity over time

- will have a different sensory profile from that of ASC children. For example, sensory issues can change according to exposure, such as ASC adults are less likely to be in crowded places like classrooms and may be able to choose to avoid sensory overwhelming situations more easily than children with ASC (Sokhadze *et al.* 2012; Casanova 2007; Casanova, Buxhoeveden and Brown 2002)

- will have different language and mobility issues from ASC children

- will (hopefully) have been given the time and the opportunity to have moved from struggling to come to terms with who they are to being in a place of acceptance (Wylie, Lawson and Beardon 2015).

After retirement for the ASC population

After retirement, many people move to new environments away from well-known structures and routines. In the non-ASC, or NT, population, retirement is often planned for, anticipated and welcomed. But for those of us in the ASC population this period of life is poorly understood. Individuals, and those caring for us, are often ill-prepared for this season of our lives.

The post-retirement years for many older people with ASC mean living in our own homes with support, in a retirement village, in an aged-care facility or in a special-needs facility. Wherever we live, we will need support specific to people with ASC.

Although we all need support as we age, typical support (physical aids for walking, hearing aids and spectacles, domestic support, health support, help to access paperwork and so on) will not be adequate on its own for older people with ASC. Older people with ASC need further support because of differing communication needs, such as: not using language to communicate; difficulties reading body language; problems of forgetting; and different sensory connections to physical, mental and emotional changes (e.g. laughter where others might cry, or not being open to reasoning due to not connecting to the information when presented orally).

Older people with ASC need guidance to understand what it means to move beyond being at work or at home. We need to understand why it is useful to look after our health, budget, home, sleep and social connections. So, although this is true for everyone, as older people with ASC we access and accommodate the information to build understanding in ways that our autism allows, not in typical terms. These are briefly outlined below but will be explored further in this book.

Assistance older people with ASC may require

Examples of things older people with ASC may require assistance with include:

- processing information (e.g. allowing extra time, avoiding metaphorical language, using visuals, using digital technology)

- setting up routines (help to replace old systems and routines with new ones)

- adapting to changes in physical wellbeing (e.g. not noticing physical decline and needing help with this)

- adapting to changing domestic needs (e.g. needing help with paperwork, arranging appointments, organising home duties)

- guidance and support with daily communication issues (e.g. not reading faces or body language typically and taking what is said literally. This may mean we need an interpreter!).

Being an older person with ASC creates specific support needs that children with ASC will not have. Children need early intervention to build language and communication skills and a sense of 'other'. For older people with ASC these most likely will already be established so it is more common that communication styles and personality profiles impact interactions within the demands of ageing. Although being autistic means we do not communicate or process information in a typical way at any age (e.g. difficulty reading information from a person's eyes, voice intonation or body language), ageing compounds these issues, presenting an individual as being one age physically but often much younger socially and emotionally (Lawson 2011).

Many of us with ASC avoid eye contact (Klin *et al.* 2003). We do this to focus on listening. Therefore we often don't register body language or access 'the big picture'. With children diagnosed with ASC, early intervention may help them build social skills to read social situations better. Similarly, assisting older people with ASC to learn the social skills needed for changes as they age is also helpful. This assistance should include guidance around understanding social context. Without understanding context, social skills become merely learnt 'robotic' behaviour that does not hold meaning for the individual. Lack of meaning often translates to incapacity to generalise. This process of building understanding cannot be delivered *en masse*. It is a personal journey that needs to be tailored to an individual's life.

There is some evidence to suggest that, with ageing, some people with ASC may experience brain changes that actually make it easier to read faces (Dickstein *et al.* 2013). This has positive implications for communication and will be discussed later.

Older people on the autism spectrum: A varying population

Autism is a spectrum of varying ability. Many of the issues covered by this book address specific needs of caring for an aged person with ASC who is high-functioning, as well as the needs of those ageing ASC individuals who are more cognitively challenged (often referred to as low-functioning with an intellectual disability). Tonge, Dissanayake and Brereton (1994) suggest that, for children with ASC, 70 per cent were intellectually challenged and 30 per cent were of average or above average intelligence. In 2013, evidence suggests that these figures have not changed and that IQ is stable across time (Howlin 2013). However, some argue that due to early intervention for children with ASC, which is enabling more opportunities for developing language and cognition, IQ can increase (Dawson *et al.* 2010). If this is the case, then future older people with ASC may have different needs from those of the older people with ASC today.

Even without intervention, many ASC individuals who were considered non-verbal as children develop language as they get older (e.g. Kanner 1943; Attwood 2008). Therefore, with today's greater levels of early intervention, it is likely that in the future a higher percentage of ageing individuals with ASC will use spoken language compared with children with ASC (e.g. Wodka, Mathy and Kalb 2013).

Even though language is often more available in ASC as one ages, this group potentially has higher stress support needs. Older people with high-functioning ASC are very aware of their communication difficulties and have insight into the impact of their behaviour, yet this does not change their autism. But, as you might imagine, it does create stress! The stress often looks to others like 'challenging behaviour' and is often misguidedly treated as such, rather than behaviour of an individual who is stressed and requires support.

Being able to talk is one thing; it doesn't necessarily mean you can utilise the associated skills. Even when a person is verbal and can 'talk', processing and utilising speech to enable typical daily interaction can be out of reach due to competing demands, which can make managing daily life problematic. For example, one study found that many of the young adults in the high-IQ group have trouble with day-to-day living – they may struggle to decide how to spend money or when to get a haircut or change their clothes, for instance (Geggel 2014). Although this study was about young adults with ASC, without appropriate support these difficulties continue into later adult life. Understanding this helps us develop appropriate services for our ageing ASC population whether or not they use verbal language.

Health challenges can go unrecognised when individuals do not notice them or are not able to tell you how they feel. As well, the residential needs of people with an ASC may be different from those found within the general population. For example, what of being lonely, liking alone time *and* wanting social contact, but not knowing how to go about bringing these successfully into your life?

Among all of the challenges associated with ageing, one potentially positive aspect is being investigated – hormonal influences in ageing ASC individuals differ from those seen in the typical population. For example, older people with ASC experiencing physical and mental decline may become more connected emotionally, compared with their NT peers. Research on the ageing brain is finding that individuals with ASC may be protected from some of the typical decline seen in the NT population due to hyperplasticity and consequential hormonal variance. For example, it appears that some brain activity in individuals with autism does not change in the same way as in typically ageing people. The ASC brain may actually offer some positive protection not seen in typical development (Oberman and Pascual-Leone 2014).

★ ★ ★

This book aims to enable carers and professionals to prepare for the tidal wave of older people with ASC needing care. It covers actions that could be approached differently and aspects that could be viewed differently for older people with ASC.

Making life better for older people with ASC makes life better for us all. Through an understanding and tolerant approach we can build a future worth looking forward to. This book will help to inform and equip people ageing with ASC and their support networks.

CHAPTER 1

Stress Support Needs

Introduction

This chapter explores why change is particularly difficult for older people living with ASC and how best to manage the associated issues that change throws up.

Forgetting is a big part of ageing. But there is some evidence which shows that individuals with ASC find it much harder to forget than neurotypical (NT) individuals do (Attwood 2008; Belmonte *et al.* 2004; Ecker *et al.* 2011; Oberman and Pascual-Leone 2014).[1]

According to research (Gomot *et al.* 2008; Gomot and Wicker 2012; Oberman and Pascual-Leone 2014), people with ASC live with a brain governed by hyperplasticity (extra plasticity). Unlike the NT brain, which decreases in plasticity as it ages, the opposite happens in ASC. This has all sorts of implications for the ASC population. For example, on the negative side there is possible trouble forgetting and, therefore, difficulty building concepts to enable forgiving. But, on the positive side, protection against developing Alzheimer's disease is a real possibility.

---

1   See also www.medical-hypotheses.com/article/S0306-9877(14)00236-9/abstract?cc=y?cc=y.

Being post-retirement age with ASC means being over the age of sixty, having poor social and conversation skills and tending to only talk about or engage with things of interest. We may have an amazing memory, though! This memory isn't only for the past, as is seen in the NT aged population, but for all manner of things that happen, including short-term memory, working memory and long-term memory.

Of course, having poor short-term memory may be an individual issue due to comorbidity, such as learning difficulties and/or attention deficit disorder (ADD). There is some evidence that poor auditory processing (due to delays and problems with the hippocampus) has a negative impact on memory. Anxiety and other sensory sensitivities will also impact memory because individuals who are anxious, nervous and unhappy will not focus well on information gathering, processing, retaining or retrieving (Boddaert *et al.* 2003).

As we age, changes to one's routine, family interaction, lifestyle, health and personal circumstances are very common. In an individual with ASC, with a mind that remembers rather than forgets and is so single-minded, these changes are experienced as a threat and can be very frightening. Understandably, then, changes for ASC individuals are dramatic and not often handled well by those experiencing them.

We can draw on research and personal stories from three areas to understand the aptitude for change of an older person with ASC. These areas are:

- the autism spectrum in general
- stress identification in ASC
- stress support needs (previously thought of as challenging behaviours).

The autism spectrum: A spectrum of ability, different ability, and disability

Because ASC is a spectrum disability (a wide range of ability, difference of ability, and disability), its impact upon ageing will vary. The influence on an individual's abilities can range from minor social difficulties and/or disability to difficulties that totally rule a person's life. On a day-to-day basis, such difficulties can come and go according to the type and level of demand upon the individual. Examples of demand include: expectations to partake in conversation (especially in an already noisy environment); making decisions, even worse when you're tired; trying to process information at a pace that others manage but might be too fast; trying to cope with unexpected change; being caught out by literality of statements that were not meant to be taken literally...to name only a few. This causes fluctuating capacity, which is hard to read and accept for both the individual and their carers.

Capacity also fluctuates between individuals. People with ASC are often referred to as being high- or low-functioning. I dislike these terms because they stigmatise individuals and are often inaccurate in describing ability and areas of difficulty. However, I use such terminology in this book to illustrate the scope of the autism spectrum. In my mind these terms translate more into descriptions such as 'requiring little support', 'requiring support' or 'requiring lots of support'. How those working with us view who we are also impacts upon what they expect of us:

- *High-functioning.* If we are high-functioning, good with language and appear to communicate well, others may place higher demands upon us than we are able to process. On the other hand, if a person is thought of as eccentric, a little strange, unusual, a genius, a bit difficult or an entrepreneur, their possible ASC may even be missed.

- *Low-functioning.* Someone with cognitive challenges and learning disability may be socially incapacitated, have huge stress support needs and may not be able to care for themselves or be left on their own.

Both of these, and everything in between, can be found in the ageing ASC population.

It is important to appreciate that both non-verbal and intellectually challenged individuals (low-functioning) *and* those with little difficulty with spoken language (seemingly higher functioning) remain daily challenged by autism and the daily demands of society (Collignon *et al.* 2013; Lawson 2011). In aged care these two groups might be sharing the same facilities, the same staff team and the same daily schedules. Clearly, the expertise needed to work with one group should be different from that needed for the other group. Further exploration of these differences is found later on in this book.

Stress identification

Once stressors are identified, a management plan can be activated, implemented, monitored and evaluated, preferably with the involvement of the individuals themselves. In other words, all programmes of care must be person-centred. It should never be assumed that if an individual doesn't use spoken language then they must have an intellectual difficulty so cannot convey their needs. If speech is absent, it does not automatically follow that cognitive ability is absent, too.

In ASC, where the brain has difficulties with communication in general due to connectivity problems,[2] the part of the language centre concerned with processing language appears to show definite differences to the development seen in neurotypicals, which causes difficulties with processing. This helps to explain the language processing issues that are seen more commonly in ASC than in typical development (Schneider 2011). Actually, the issues are more to do with connectivity between the senses and the ability to process language, which leads to an auditory processing issue rather than a sensory or physical issue. Then again, it has been found that both over-connectivity and under-connectivity occur in people with ASC and, according to the patterns for specific individuals, the difficulties and benefits will alter (Hahamy, Behrmann and Malach 2014).

Connectivity is separate to cognition. For example, an individual may have the usual ability to think, reason, and form ideas and associations but not have connections to the words to express them. In the NT population these abilities are found in shared domains but in ASC they may not be. In ASC there is evidence that messages between synapses tend to connect in one direction rather than many and this means that messages get lost.

---

2   See http://minicolumn.org/people/casanova.

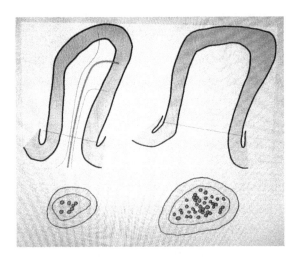

Less connectivity occurring due to shorter connections between neurons and spacing between and within mini-columns than in typical development (Casanova 2011)

This difficulty can be very frustrating in older ASC individuals because they may be fully aware (unlike children with ASC) of the expectations being placed upon them but not able to explain why they cannot comply. It is even worse for such an individual when one assumes that they are less able due to lack of speech – they may fully understand but not be able to tell you so in conventional terms. Schneider's (2011) research indicates that the centres for language in ASC look and operate differently for an older person with autism than might be the case for a child with ASC. However, this difference is yet to be fully investigated. Schneider's research with an older female (over the age of 60) on the autism spectrum, who was also an academic in the world of animal science, showed why language and words are so difficult to process in ASC.[3]

In ASC, speech often interferes with processing and, therefore, needs to be used sparingly. But there are many other ways to facilitate communication that do not require the use of words. Sometimes gestures and signing can be used, sometimes photographs and images, sometimes the use of augmented and/or facilitated communication is needed (e.g. the use of a keyboard, digital tablet and appropriate software that aids communication, such as Proloquo2Go supplied by iTunes). By whichever means, the individual needs to be at the centre of the planning, even if plans are explored by means other than language for those pre-verbal individuals sometimes considered low-functioning.

Challenging behaviour

It can appear as though many older individuals with ASC are not listening or not able to connect, especially socially and emotionally, or are only focused on things they choose. People caring for older people with ASC could misjudge this behaviour for stubbornness or being difficult. While the behaviour is not voluntary or easily changed, it can be managed by trained personnel who understand the person and have strategies to deal with certain situations. A colleague of mine once commented on how difficult it would be living with 'the inability to forget' (Attwood 2003).

The ASC brain's single-mindedness (e.g. Brandwein *et al.* 2013) combined with an inability to forget work together to keep ASC individuals hooked into the past, but linked

---

3   See www.lrdc.pitt.edu/schneiderlab.

with the present. For example, instructions given by all dark-haired men in their thirties may go unheeded because, years earlier, one dark-haired young man failed to turn up on time. This combination can blur timelines and cause difficulty with separation of events, times, places and people:

> ...too much plasticity may lead to instability of structural connections and compromise of functional systems necessary for cognition and behaviour. (Oberman and Pascual-Leone 2014, p.3)

To compensate for the 'over-connection' leading to processing difficulties, we must provide the structure, routine, order and schedules that illustrate current time and separate it from the past. This is one way to keep an individual connected to real time.

When changes to routine occur without warning and without our involvement it can feel as if we have been uprooted from all we know and placed in a dark room without windows. It is more than uncomfortable; it is painful and frightening (Lawson 2011; Mukaetova-Ladinska *et al.* 2011). Yet change of one kind or another is a daily occurrence for all of us and we need to know how to adapt and/or cope.

We older people with ASC experience an exaggerated effect of being single-minded (e.g. Belmonte 2000; Collignon *et al.* 2013) because our ASC means we are already single-focused and then ageing increases the effect and causes our brains to have even further trouble in multi-tasking. One of the reasons older individuals with ASC are even more pedantic about things of interest to them is that they are not able to relate outside of that interest. (This is not their choice so much as an autism disposition born from a brain wired to work through one sense at a time.)

Often, this behaviour is met with suspicion as though ASC individuals are stubbornly ignoring the rest of the world. This can be really disconcerting because family, friends and carers treat them in a way that they don't understand.

Yet, when ASC individuals are motivated and interest is sparked, their attention is captured. This connects to meaning in an open channel, enhancing attention and leading to their window of attention being broadened. It is possible for older people with ASC to focus on more than one thing at a time, but only when motivated. This is the default setting in ASC, unlike the ability to multi-task, even outside of interest, in the typical population (Lawson 2011).

Being aged and ASC will mean being someone who might not cope well with change unless they are given a new way to accommodate the changes and form new routines. These must be founded on their skills and strengths. This leads to motivation.

In aged-care facilities, such routines and structures come with the territory. But often, just as an individual gets used to the weekly routine, changes occur. Managers may believe that variety is good for the soul, or keeping routines the same will cause individuals to be bored. Obviously, menus, staffing and activities all change over time as a matter of course. But familiarity and established routine allow older people with ASC a sense of security as we can relax in knowing what to expect. Take these away and we are lost. Forward thinking is a multi-task operation. We are not designed for this unless it occurs within an area of interest.

If there has to be a change in the expected routine then pre-warning of such a change is very important. A visual, auditory or kinaesthetic reminder, according to what suits the individual best, can work well. Examples include a daily newsletter with space for amendments, a spoken instruction on CD or an actual acted-out instruction for those who need to do, not just see or hear it. The cues need to support the idea of change, but not cause the individual to become anxious. It could be a text message sent to a mobile phone or a personal message delivered by a carer. A visual activities calendar, with Velcro interchangeable pictures and words that can easily be swapped over if necessary, may work for some. These Velcro pictures always sit at the base of the calendar so the individual is aware that change can happen, and is prepared for it.

Recognising issues of 'change' in ASC

Older people living with ASC may not even be aware that significant changes are happening within their own bodies. Yet, being cognisant of the change is only half the battle. It may also be very difficult to figure out what to do about the changes. Once one has worked out what to do, addressing each issue appropriately needs to be explored and practised step by step, separating issues such as personal and physical changes, menu changes, staff changes, social changes and so on.

Unlike the NT population, who are better at multi-tasking because they are designed to divide attention, older people with ASC may stay stuck in time (Harmon 2010; Lawson 2011). Noting the issues and then exploring what to do about them (multi-tasking) is very challenging and leads to an increase in stress.

Other areas where change is a concern and will impact negatively upon the older person with ASC include:

- physical health (e.g. being in pain but not able to tell someone)

- family communication (e.g. not being consulted)
- relationship pressures (e.g. loss of a loved one; changes to family dynamics)
- mental health (e.g. dealing with mood changes associated with hormones; depression and changes in libido).

Depression, isolation and premature death are very prevalent issues for older people with ASC, as some of the individual stories in this book indicate. Again, these occur more frequently than with older NT people because the individual will not be good at problem-solving typically.

Discomfort with change in one's circumstances is common to us all, but individuals with social awareness can communicate their discomfort and explore problem-solving options. They can problem-solve typically, using thought-processing and verbal skills (self-talk, talking to others). It is relatively easy for them to use a telephone, arrange meetings, budget and understand financial matters, share issues with friends, organise, know what is at stake, and so on.

These are normal NT social skills that do not occur naturally in older ASC individuals. For many, ageing with ASC will mean taking things literally, struggling with reading or not being able to read between the lines, not being good at understanding metaphor and possibly not able to connect or verbalise one's thoughts, feelings or needs. Because of these traits, ageing ASC individuals will be susceptible to abuse and mistreatment.

The ASC brain compared with the NT brain

Research is finding that older people with ASC continue to learn and that the brain is more 'plastic' than in the typical ageing population (e.g. Dickstein *et al.* 2013). There is evidence that difficulties with face recognition in children with ASC become less so in older people with ASC (e.g. Dickstein *et al.* 2013). This has implications for communication with the ageing population of ASC individuals. Although communication difficulties are based on much more than reading facial expressions, there may be opportunities for increased face recognition in older people with ASC, enabling higher social skills due to there being one less hurdle to navigate!

In ASC, the brain is configured to work with single focus, routines and interest (American Psychiatric Association 2013). When individuals are drawn away from a routine, or a routine is interrupted, focus is lost and it is very difficult to refocus (Belmonte *et al.* 2004). Because ASC individuals don't think and process information typically, offering typical solutions won't work (e.g. time to adjust; telling someone that routine changes are good). If this type of routine destruction happens often then depression may ensue. Once depression takes root it is difficult to deal with because, although the symptoms look similar to depression in NT individuals, they are experienced via a different window.

ASC individuals tend to think *or* feel, one at a time, rather than combining these skills. It is more one-channelled rather than both occurring simultaneously (Attwood 2008; Kalbe *et al.* 2010; Lawson 2011). For example, during conversation faces are so expressive that they distract individuals with ASC. So people with ASC have to decide, *Do I watch or listen?* This is why those of us with ASC so often don't look at you when we're speaking or being spoken to. We can only do one thing at a time.

Unlike information processed by the NT population (where thoughts and feelings are connected), the mind–feelings battle can cause the older person with ASC to get 'stuck' in their thoughts *or* in their feelings; rumination or 'the washing machine effect' results. It's like having the needle stuck in the groove of a long-playing record; that section of the record plays over and over and over again. There is no relief from these thoughts or feelings.

Individuals can be helped to break free from this rumination by learning to use cognitive behavioural therapy (CBT). CBT challenges the individual's thinking to create a new emotive state. Others might use a type of acceptance and commitment therapy (ACT). This is where individuals are taught how to become mindful of the present (their breathing, posture, surroundings, and so on), and rather than challenging their thinking they learn to accept and embrace it. There is evidence that such therapy causes the brain to reduce anxiety and this helps the rumination to decrease.[4]

Older people with ASC who are not able to participate in CBT or ACT due to cognitive status (being low-functioning) will need different assistance to help them out of the groove of their thinking or emotions. They may need to be motivated to side-step their rumination via a stimulating interest, or shift focus via a video story, a bus trip or a meaningful relational activity, such as walking in a park or along the beach. However, distraction alone will not end the cycle permanently; it is just a temporary fix. This is because until and unless there is a

---

4   See www.actmindfully.com.au/acceptance_&_commitment_
    therapy.

reasonable conclusion to the episode (e.g. a swap from feeling sad to feeling glad because a favourite video is showing; a change in staffing; different food on the menu), the fixed belief, feeling or frustration keeps coming back.

Lack of motivation

In the NT population if the older person lacks motivation, is highly anxious, neglecting self-care, feeling loss of hope and so on, the person is likely to be aware that this is happening. If friends or family pick up on this and address the issues through conversation, the person feels heard and gains insight. They are also open to ideas that can assist them. Ideally, plans are made, action taken and support provided.

The thought processes and reasoning linked to the loss of hope, demotivation or even catatonia (inability to move) have a different foundation, expression and outcome in ASC because the brain is not wired up to connect via talking modes alone. The NT population can attend counselling and verbally challenge their thinking, so this is the usual means of assisting with a variety of mental health issues, lack of self-worth and so on, as well as the use of medication. But this might not work for those with ASC because meaning, access to verbal reasoning, thinking and exploring of emotions and cognitive processes are often unavailable, especially in low-functioning ASC. This implies that it needs to be tackled differently; for example via the mind, not only through verbal negotiation but in visual, auditory or kinaesthetic (acted out) ways.

Management plan

Any plan to manage the above needs various considerations. It is vital that all of the ideology described here is taken on board. Adaptation for individuals with ASC needs careful planning, intervention and ongoing review and maintenance. If one intervention or plan fails to work, then another needs to be trialled. Sometimes it can take a while for concepts and understanding to 'click'. Please give it time.

Preparing for retirement

Many older individuals with ASC may once have had a successful career, been an active member of the community, raised a family and, to all outward appearances, have coped well with their lives. But once they leave work, routines are often broken and this confident and apparent competency may leave. Many feel like they are lost in a desert without signposts. This happens because in ASC the brain is not wired typically, and multi-tasking, outside of interest and usual routines, is limited. The usual means of coping, such as talking to friends, being able to multi-task and so on, are possible for the NT population, but are often out of reach for individuals with ASC (Ecker *et al.* 2011; Gomot and Wicker 2012; Lawson 2011).

Being a member of the typical population might mean that individuals have a post-retirement plan based on looking forward to developing other interests (e.g. travel, golf, photography). Because they have a brain configured to multi-task they may have several different interests. This is a time to be excited. If a typical individual is depressed at the loss of their usual job and routine, and feels somehow less valued, then they can be supported to see their potential. Conversation can be a medium for building connections and systems for the type of support the individual needs.

If, however, this is the only way support is offered, the ASC individual may simply switch off as words may fail to build the kind of picture they need (e.g. Happé and Frith 2006).

Plan implementation: Motivation

For ageing ASC individuals, a management plan will involve finding a way to work with them to problem-solve. First the individual has to be motivated and then, through a single interest that is important to them (e.g. gardening, map reading or painting), a plan can be constructed.

If gardening is an interest and is motivating, for example, one can demonstrate visually why the garden – which could represent one's life – needs tending. (Although metaphor is often difficult to grasp for people with ASC, when interest is triggered metaphor is more accessible.) Gardening can represent what to do in which season (time, event, season of one's life), how to do this and which tools are needed. Using gardening as motivation and explanation also connects the individual because it turns the brain 'on' (connects ideas and concepts) and is using language from where the individual lives (their passion or obsession).

All of the above can act as a way of building connections for older people with ASC. For example, using knowledge about the seasons that a garden grows through can be helpful in explaining the seasons an individual might go through. Explaining the need for different clothing, different modes of transport, meals and entertainment can all be explored via the gardening metaphor.

If gardening isn't of interest then it is not helpful to use this as a metaphor. Instead, the individual may relate to cooking and recipes or to a specific television programme. Whatever it is, using these as metaphors for life can make the difference between building understanding or leaving a person in the dark.

Plan implementation: Developing new routines

ASC individuals must be motivated about everything, from merely functioning to completing activities well. Motivation switches the brain on and creates a pathway to building connections through a brain wavelength known as gamma. Gamma is the brain wavelength that connects messages from other brain-wave information to give a more rounded 'picture' of what is being perceived. It appears that when an older person with ASC is motivated, gamma is triggered and does its job of taking information from other brain waves, such as beta and theta, to enable a fuller picture to be seen or experienced (Lawson 2013). In ASC, outside of motivation, gamma lies in excess, therefore doesn't work as it should and is not able to do its job efficiently:

> The ability to engage socially depends upon being able to attend (notice) physical, cognitive, emotional and sensory aspects of 'self' and of 'other'. This activity depends upon gamma connectivity. Gamma connectivity is powered down in ASC but can be artificially remedied via motivation. (Lawson 2013, p.1)

Looking at certain aspects of the aged brain in ASC we see a picture like the one below (Lawson 2011, 2013; see also Brown *et al.* 2010).[5]

---

5   Also see www.sfari.org/news-and-opinion/news/2013/autism-brains-marked-by-weak-local-connections-study-says.

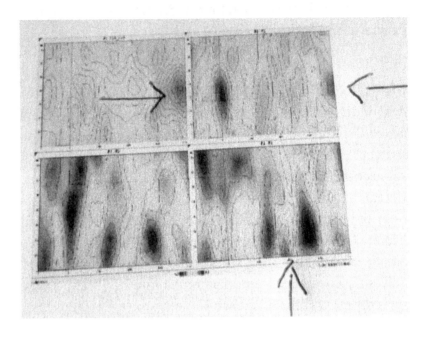

Typical gamma pattern in an individual with ASC

Certain patches shown indicate that gamma is in excess in ASC (e.g. Lawson 2013).

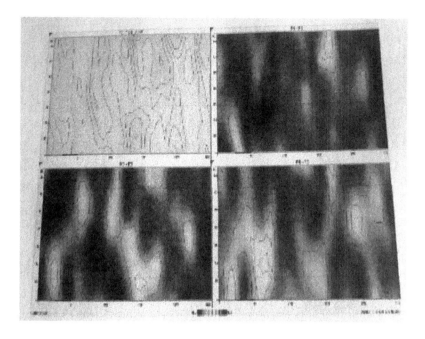

Typical gamma pattern in an NT individual

In the image above, gamma is working effectively in a typical brain by 'mixing' information appropriately, so an individual can make sense of it. The gamma is blended so we don't see it. The fact that gamma is not doing its job efficiently in the ASC brain partly accounts for verbal processing being slower in individuals with ASC than in the NT population. Because of the slower response time with ASC individuals, they may appear to be hearing-impaired. Of course, raising the volume of one's voice does not solve this problem. Shouting at the ASC person can cause sensory overload so the individual becomes very stressed. They may cover their ears, scream louder to block the other voice or walk away. Because conversational instructions are difficult to process, the content will be missed or it will take longer to process.

Ways around this difficulty with verbal processing may include the use of visuals, such as a picture calendar, and, more generally, replacing words with pictures (Grandin 2006). It is also important to understand an individual's learning style (e.g. visual, auditory, kinaesthetic). People who doodle while on the telephone, for example, are visual and tactile learners. Others would rather you spoke your phone number out loud while they type the numbers into their own phone rather than have you write it out for them to copy. This implies they are not visual learners but auditory learners. Visuals can actually get in the way of how auditory learners process information best.

Once staff and other carers get to know each person's learning style, all plans concerning them can be presented in ways that make sense to that individual. For example, some older people with ASC need written information rather than spoken, whilst others prefer spoken information rather than written. This may be different for the individual from when they were a child because then they didn't do so well with words or they had problems reading facial expressions. Appropriate interventions need to change over time as individuals age.

Monitoring and evaluating ASC behaviour

Staff and carers supporting low-functioning older people with ASC often notice behaviour that is distressing. This may be rocking, flapping, humming or pacing, or it may be behaviour that is sexually inappropriate, for example inordinate affection. It is assumed that such behaviour is of a mental, emotional or cognitive disposition rather than physical. However, issues expressed emotionally or via behaviour may actually stem from physical causes. Recognising the root cause of any behaviour (as physical, mental, emotional or cognitive) is not an easy task but it is an extremely important one. As a matter of course all physical explanations must be explored (e.g. pain, discomfort, illness) and addressed or treated. Only then can the possible emotional or mental reasons for the behaviour be explored (e.g. is the person upset, excited, tired and/or overwhelmed)?

Case study: Myself

As I've aged, I've noticed a few changes related to ASC that are relevant to this discussion. I've divided them into physical setting, emotional wellbeing and social setting, though clearly each overlap.

Physical setting
This broad topic includes health and mobility at home, outside home, at work, using public transport, and visiting family and friends.

As I've become older the sensory issues I live with have worsened. The impact on me of noise (from conversation, TV, radio), clutter (too much stuff in the room, or on a shelf), physical demands (walking, bending, feeding my cats) and the expectation that I can multi-task (look and listen at the same time) have all increased. They can be more overwhelming and leave me more tired and irritable than when I was younger. The need for order has also increased as I have aged. This is because when things are ordered there is less demand on my processing abilities. If things get 'out of order' it almost immobilises me.

Just like any other ageing individual I have increased mobility issues as my knees and back have become very arthritic. Living with ASC and ageing makes simple transport strategies more difficult than for non-ASC ageing individuals. For example, if I need to take public transport or ride a taxi, the chatter from others, having the radio on and the bus bell are all difficult to cope with because they require joint attention, which is too demanding for me. I wish I could 'turn them off'. Sometimes I don't go out into the community even to shop for things I need because I can't control, and therefore fear, the outside physical environment. When I do venture outside, I often need earplugs or a head-set or I go at times when town and shops are less busy so there are fewer people and less demand on me. These take the edge off noise and make going out a bearable task.

Sight loss, hearing loss and loss of strength or stamina to do things is becoming more noticeable, which is very depressing. These ailments also mean I need more visits to the doctor and hospital. If, as ASC ageing individuals, we have to go to a hospital for any surgical procedure this must be clearly planned, explained and executed.

In general the difficulty for people with ASC relates to forward thinking and our tendency to be very literal. The whole doctor/hospital event will be fraught with difficulty. What will it mean if our appointment time says one thing but we are not warned that this is only a guide? What if medical staff don't appreciate that an ASC individual may be tactile defensive and will be extremely upset if someone attempts to touch them?

All concepts need to be explained to individuals and to their supporters. Follow-up plans must also be clearly spelt out. For some people, putting these into words may not be adequate communication. Individuals might do better with a story, pictures (Kana *et al.* 2006) and even video to explain what is likely to happen. I love making short video messages as I process information, remind myself of appointments or just record an event. If I wish I can email these to myself and to others.

Emotional wellbeing

In general I do better with space and quietness. Also, I need support from people who help by explaining concepts and what's about to happen. My emotional wellbeing often depends upon my being able to attend to things that interest me. For example, I can be heard laughing to myself as I watch the antics of the colourful parrots in my garden.

Even though I have a PhD and will happily give a lecture or facilitate a workshop, I still need support crossing busy roads, getting the shopping done or filling in forms for authorities. I also need clear explanations of what might be happening to/for me and for others. This can be presented via social video stories or sharing concerns via TV programmes. (For example, Google and YouTube are great, because they don't have overwhelming facial expressions or body language.) These two-dimensional images seem to require less processing than three-dimensional interaction, while at the same time offering all the information I need.

I need to rest and have time away from emotional demand. Without this I can become moody, less communicative and more likely to react in negative ways to demands, such as through fatigue or headaches. This might seem like a common issue for anyone, but the size of the response will be different from that seen in older NT individuals. For example, older people with ASC might simply close down and not be able to tell you what's happening. Some might become loud, aggressive or totally withdrawn.

Social setting

Some of us really need other people in our lives on a daily basis, but their presence needs to be structured into our day and not thrust suddenly upon us. The older I get the more I need these structures and routines. It's not like in typical older people needing the occasional reminder or liking to sit on the same comfy chair. My need for structure extends to clothing, what I eat, my TV viewing, what I say and in what order things need to be done. If it's not done exactly to routine many of us can be upset (close off to all communication) for the entire day. It's as if we needed 'that thing' in order to know what 'the next thing' is.

I don't need as much social contact as some might, and I like time to myself. This need for quiet time has increased as I have gotten older. Again, the difference for me compared with an older NT is that I might last ten minutes over a coffee and a chat before I notice my senses shutting down. Then I'll get up and move away. There isn't time for explanations or small talk. Even a small amount of 'social' can be overwhelming. It can cause my mind to feel as if it's going to explode! Needing a clear beginning and a clear ending to social situations is important to helping us cope.

Doing 'social' is very tiring and I'm not being anti-social when I request limited interaction with a group (even family). I require more time to process social interaction, and more time to recover from social activity, than a typical older person.

Fewer difficulties for some?

For some, moving through the spectrum as we age will mean experiencing fewer difficulties as a result of their autism than when they were younger. For example, some elderly ASC individuals are more at home in their skin, are set up in their homes and are very capable in their relationships. They have things worked out. But this may change dramatically if their ageing presents challenges that mean they can no longer care for themselves without support.

Unseen difficulties

One older ASC individual spoke to me of her fears that she was not coping with the domestics of running a home (cleaning, bill-paying, washing, shopping) and she knew she needed home help from her local council. This meant having another person in her home for two hours twice a week. She was terrified at the thought of having a person in her home who would not understand her autism, might expect conversation and would not go about things in the order or way that she was used to. This fear prevented her from seeking help. Life became more and more difficult as her bills, washing and cleaning mounted up. She still managed to feed herself because she ordered her groceries online.

When this happens to NT individuals they may not like the changes but they will understand why it's happening, what this might mean and where to seek support (e.g. council, community centre, general practitioner).

Summary

This chapter has explored the reasons for 'challenging behaviours' concerned with stress support needs, related to memory changes and 'change' in general. Later in the book, Chapter 7 explores the idea of 'challenges' from the angle of sensory dysphoria (sensory issues).

⚑ Key points

- Structure and routine are vital, helping older people with ASC connect to real time and enabling them to cope better with change.

- Planning, intervention and ongoing maintenance help us adapt to change.

- Non-invasive communications are useful and can include a daily newsletter with a section for amendments, text message sent to a mobile phone or a personal message delivered by a carer, a visual activities calendar or notice board. These are easier to process and accommodate rather than, for example, sudden announcements over a loudspeaker coming through the ceiling in our care home room!

- Fluctuating capacity is the norm for older people with ASC.

- High-functioning autism requires support in ways that may not be obvious.

- Low-functioning autism requires more daily support at every level (e.g. communication needs, support with activities, appropriate sexuality, turn-taking).

- Older people with ASC have more elasticity in their brains, making face recognition easier with age and leading to a disposition to remember rather than forget.

- When changes to timetabled activities, menu or staff occur, older people with ASC can believe this is terminal and this can cause them to close off all communication.

- Programmes should be put together with ASC individuals at the centre. When making decisions about older people with ASC, a good rule of thumb is: *Nothing about me without me.*

Stress support needs can be well managed through developing new routines, improving motivation and communicating effectively. Building and maintaining good communication strategies is the subject of Chapter 2.

Building Appropriate Communication Strategies

Introduction

Whether the ASC individual is living at home or in aged care, management plans need to be activated, implemented, monitored and evaluated, as discussed in Chapter 1. Any ideas and all plans need to be communicated, and communication involving ASC can be quite a challenge.

All that accompanies getting old, with all of the physical, financial, emotional and personal implications for ASC individuals, needs to be communicated in ways that make sense to that individual. For older people with ASC different issues will need to be communicated in different ways according to individual needs, personalities, learning styles, cognitive ability, social skills, mental and physical health and so on.

This chapter explores the communication challenge and looks at communication styles and strategies.

Communication

Communication is an exchange that involves giving and receiving information. We need to establish checks and balances, such as recording information, conducting appropriate meetings between all concerned, and being accountable. This helps to ensure that the ASC individual can both give and receive timely and accurate information.

Staff, carers and older people with ASC themselves need to develop communication skills relevant to both personality and situation. A good place to start is to gain a clear understanding of how ASC is impacting each individual. This process may not be easy when the older people with ASC find it more difficult than their neurotypical (NT) peers to know and understand themselves. Generally, we assume that with age comes wisdom, knowledge and the ability to know when, where, how often, who with and in what situations such knowledge and wisdom can and should be used. Living with ASC can cloud judgement, keep the individual single-minded and often make reasoning quite difficult. Therefore, the best communication strategies are those that are not typical (e.g. not language-based alone) and have the ASC individual on-side. This will mean getting to know the individual, using communication strategies based on their skills, strengths and interests, and working with their learning styles.

Communication strategies

For those of us with ASC, sensory systems work best when processing one thing at a time rather than several things at once. Therefore, looking at a person at the same time as listening to them is very difficult and uncomfortable. We attend to either one or the other, not both at once. Yet, so often, the person with whom we are communicating feels unheard or unimportant if we don't look at them during conversation. Also, in this fast-paced world, ASC individuals can find it hard to keep up and/or be heard because other people don't allow enough processing time. This is especially difficult if any distractions are present, such as music, groups of people or traffic.

How does an older person with ASC who has average IQ explain the difficulties they are experiencing when talking, looking, reading faces, listening and so on, while, at the same time, dealing with these distracting issues? Understanding that ASC individuals can cope well within their passion, interest or expertise, but that these skills may not generalise across other domains, takes the community some way to appreciating the difficulties that older people with ASC live with. We can do many things when interested because interest focuses our abilities but, outside of our passion, we struggle. Unfortunately those supporting us see our abilities in one area and assume we are being lazy or difficult when we don't generalise these abilities to other areas.

Making adaptations and concessions for an individual who is blind or in a wheelchair is seen as a legitimate need; it is part of caring for them. It is necessary to do the same for older people with ASC. This is a three-fold process:

1. Learn about ASC.

2. Get to know the individual, including the particular traits of their ASC.

3. Devise communication plans based on a sound understanding of the above, plus the individual's unique personality and learning styles (see Chapter 3).

Many high-functioning ASC people have held down good jobs during their younger years. They may have been politicians, doctors, teachers, in the armed forces, management, catering, the arts and sciences, media, academia, the care industry or real estate. In fact they are in most professions, especially where systems and structure are essential to the workplace or employment. Yet, even within these situations, where they managed their employment necessities so well, they may have had issues with social interactions and daily decisions, such as when or what to eat. Because they work so well at what they do well, these 'difficulties' can get put to one side and they either 'fake it to make it', develop great 'masking skills' or just live with the difficulties. In fact, high-functioning females in particular with ASC tend to be better at 'acting' or mimicking NT profiles. This makes it much harder to recognise the difficulties they live with.

Individuals with ASC are less likely to fit well into jobs that require quick changes to routine, such as vocations requiring spontaneous decisions and work that depends upon versatility and adaptability. It is no different for us during our ageing years, except that (because we may no longer be the ones in charge or able to operate from the structures we once knew) we may need support in our everyday lives with ordinary things such as choosing what to eat from a menu or where to sit at table. These daily activities may not be factored into the structure of our ordinary lives because carers might believe they need to leave it up to us.

Making a choice

Choice, however, is best left to decisions between only a couple of things, and these need specifying; for example, 'Vegemite or marmalade on your toast?'

Carers need to check in with each older person with ASC in their care. Maybe they need a visual timetable that clearly shows the daily expectations, the comings and goings of any staff supporting them, the leisure activities, meal plans and so on. Carers also need to work out if it is enough just to tell someone what the expectations are or whether the person needs the information written down as well. There are a variety of ways to communicate information, but even when typical language is used, metaphor and literalness can be a problem. For example, why tell someone you'll be 'a minute' if you mean you'll be ten?

Living with ASC as older individuals is to live with a diff-ability or difference of ability that shows up in how we understand the world and in how we communicate. Although this behaviour is typical in autism at any age, the effect it has on an older person with ASC needs consideration.

Communication of high-functioning older people with ASC is not 'disordered' so much as it might be inappropriate or mistimed. We find it hard to read social signs (e.g. body language, facial expression, tone of voice) but there will be an expectation upon us that we should understand these by now. After all, we're not children any more. This being so, some of the behaviours we exhibit will be related to our difficulty with interpreting social expectation. These difficulties are often described as 'challenging behaviours'. However, the challenges that such behaviours give rise to are more to do with our being stressed and are more aptly named 'stress support needs'.

These stress support needs may not be about difficult behaviours that others find challenging, so much as they might be about needing an appropriate pair of spectacles (metaphorically speaking) to enable us to clarify the social expectations we are struggling with.

Because of our difficulty reading social expectations, some refer to autism as a state of 'mind blindness' that can lead to a lack of empathy. This implies we are unfeeling and uncaring, but that is very far from the truth. In fact, at times, we are so empathetic that it's painful. I know some ageing

ASC individuals who don't watch news programmes because they find them too distressing. So, should people think, 'Oh, autism, this means they lack empathy' or should they think, 'Reading social expectation is difficult for this person'?

Judging older ASC individuals in one or other of these ways impacts how NT people live and work with them. One way of thinking will lead to 'switching off' from an individual with ASC and possibly being less aware and less caring of their needs, in order not to be hurt by their apparent inability to respond 'typically'; and the other way of thinking will enable NT people to see the need to communicate social expectations in a way that builds 'meaning' for an individual.

If the individual is cognitively challenged due to an intellectual disability, they may need carers to convey their message in fewer words. For example, consider the mixed message of the following: 'Hi. Dinner is ready and it's on the table, so you might like to come to the table now, please.' (A lot of words to convey a minimal action and which actually offer an individual a choice – they might not like to come to the table.) Instead, what could be said is: 'Dinner. Come, sit and eat.' This might seem less polite but it actually involves less processing and is less taxing on cognitive abilities.

If an individual is quickly overloaded by demands of conversation, a carer can pass them a note, or email or text them the information instead of speaking it. For individuals who have many sensory difficulties (e.g. lights, voices, radio, television and movement from people quickly become too much), a carer needs to convey information without looking at the individual (side-on is good) in a space where there is calm, lack of clutter and no overwhelming fragrances.

Finding a 'theme' or avenue for communication

I am a science fiction fanatic. Sometimes I imagine I'm a mutant with particular strengths in certain areas and difficulties in others. This appeals to me because in many science fiction stories it is the mutants who win the day. If I thought of myself as damaged, deficient and less than 'normal' I would fail to feel valuable, important and needed. It is helpful for older people with ASC to find a niche for themselves, a place they can belong to. It might be a fictional character they identify with, a place to go to in their mind, a memory of an earlier vocation or relationship, or simply a 'state of being' they are comfortable with. My mum reads Mills and Boon romance novels. On meeting her you would not expect her to enjoy these. She has an accountant's mind; she's great with numbers, and is a formal person with quite 'black and white' logic. But these books occupy her mind and take her places that she seems to relate to and enjoy.

Case study: Living in an aged-care facility

Each Sunday, we collect my ASC mum from the aged-care facility at the end of our street and bring her home to spend most of the day with us. She enjoys her home-cooked roast dinner and a glass of sparkling wine. In the aged-care facility they do their best but Mum is just one elderly lady among so many other elderly people.

Activities to suit

Mum has specific likes and dislikes, just as any other person might. But in the aged-care facility they don't have the staff to allow Mum the same choices and rights that she had when she lived in her own home. We do our best to explain this to her but her literal thinking suggests that if it can be done, it *should* be done.

Mum, like so many of us ageing with ASC, isn't very social and does not like to mix with other people. It's a real effort for her to eat with others in the dining room. She makes herself go so that she isn't a total recluse. She knows the rule is 'go to the dining room', so, even if it was suggested she eat in her room, she would be horrified because it's 'against the rules'. It's surprising how many of the staff fail to appreciate that Mum really doesn't want to join in with the activities unless they are pre-arranged, like her card game.

Some of the activities that have worked with Mum, however, include organising a small group card game, a small group Bingo session, visits to the care facility hairdresser and podiatrist, and a weekly shoulder massage. We have told the masseur that Mum needs firm massage and for the same technique to be used each week. If one of the proposed appointments needs to be cancelled this has to be done in good time and with a definite plan of when the event will be reconvened.

Mum on the swing seat at home

Mum has false teeth that don't always stay in position. We have bought her the fixative gel that is supposed to help, but due to magnified sensory information, such as smell, touch and taste, she can't cope with the feel of it in her mouth so doesn't use it. Conversation with Mum is quite difficult because her teeth will often pop out and her speech becomes slurred. This has a negative impact on other residents and means they find it uncomfortable to be around her. She tries to chat to them but they appear to ignore her. I believe this is because of her teeth and slurred speech, but it's very difficult to explain this to her.

Mum is a coeliac and only eats certain foods. Chewing her food and choosing what she would prefer to eat are also often a problem. Even though the facility brings her a special gluten-free diet, it's not usually the type of food she likes. For example, they give her ice cream, which she doesn't like, and salads that are hard to chew! Mum would prefer a lovely shepherd's pie, a pasta dish or a curry. But so often these are not available gluten-free.

Being one of many residents, the kitchen staff can't just make Mum a special meal of her choice and so, because she doesn't like what is on offer, Mum will say she isn't hungry. We try to supplement her meals by buying her favourite biscuits and candy bars. When I bake I'll often give portions to Mum and the staff put them in the fridge for her. But, even though her name is on the package, the food disappears. It's very frustrating for Mum and for us. It can mean that Mum thinks we haven't put the items in the fridge. It's very hard to reason with and explain things to elderly ASC individuals. In many ways it's harder than trying to explain to children because an older ASC individual may have a belief system that their age gives them certain 'rights'. Discussing whether their rights have, in fact, been violated is difficult if the older person with ASC doesn't have a perception of other social concepts.

Overall, the aged-care facilities are terrific. The receptionists are great and everyone is very helpful. They do their best to make sure Mum feels safe, listened to and accommodated.

But a facility caring for nearly 400 people, with at least a hundred living with dementia, can only do so much.

Sensory overload
Each morning (except on weekends because staff are not available to facilitate this), announcements are made over the intercom. As far as Mum is concerned, a voice suddenly speaks from the ceiling in her room to let her know the day's events. The voice annoys her. It's as if each time she hears it is like the first time; she is always surprised! She wishes she could turn it off, but she can't. As a resident, she has no say in the day-to-day running of the facility. She can't even choose what happens in her own room.

Making changes

Imagine how things might look if older people living with ASC in aged-care facilities could have agency over some of the actions that so affect their daily lives. The best way for this to occur is for communication to be built up with the ASC individual as the narrator and originator of the plans. This should be a joint exercise and one that is closely monitored, together, as part of the team. No sudden announcements, no sudden changes, no sudden anything! For this type of communication to work, people caring for older people with ASC need to get to know us, relate to us in ways that make sense to us and, rather than see our behaviour as challenging and something that needs a behaviour plan, see it as a sign and symptom of stress, implying we have 'stress support needs'. This shifts the emphasis from our behaviour being a problem to our need for support in order to lower stress.

Of course, life becomes even more complicated if the older ASC individual has dementia. They may still be involved with their own care but may need constant reminders of the plans and these will need to be visited often.

Cognitive delay or intellectual disability

If I'm 70 with the emotional/cognitive/social age of a six-year-old, is it really appropriate to try to make me responsible for my own hygiene, health, daily routine and other adult pursuits? I will need 'parenting' for the rest of my life. But parenting does not mean being dictated to, it means putting my needs at the centre, keeping me safe, working with my capabilities and not allowing others to take advantage of me.

Tailoring procedures to suit the individual

Following the model *Nothing about me without me*, all care plans must be recorded and important others made aware of these plans. Plans should be documented and all involved need to be aware of preferred communication styles. Building in accountability is mandatory. All daily activities, however mundane, need to be implemented in ways that make sense. As stated earlier, these need to be visual, written, texted, emailed or put across in ways that build connection to understanding.

Case study: An individual with high-functioning ASC

Debbie received a late diagnosis of Asperger's syndrome (high-functioning autism) at 45. She's never really been in the position of being 'cared for' as a result of having Asperger's.

After leaving home in her early twenties, she moved into her own flat and got a job as a lab technician. She rarely socialised. She first became unwell with her nerves when she was about 30. Bullied at work, she became paranoid, which continued until she left that job, and was in hospital with depression for a while. She'd had a good salary, but afterwards she worked on a minimum wage and went from one job to another until she was 44. The last job she had was in a clinical hospital lab and the lab bully targeted her when her previous victim left. Her mental health is still very poor.

One of the less positive things about being over fifty for Debbie is the slowing of the rate at which her brain processes information. In the morning it takes her much longer for her brain to kick in than it used to. She feels as if she has constant 'brain fog' and gets irritable easily. She tries to tell herself to be more 'easy going', as she doesn't want to be anxious and annoyed. Her sleep is erratic. Relaxation therapies such as yoga and meditation help to calm her racing thoughts.

Relationships

The loss of Debbie's mum had a devastating effect on her. Her mum used to phone Debbie often and was always interested in what she was doing and how she was. Since she died, Debbie feels like she's bobbing about on her own in the middle of an ocean. It's as if she's watching the world and not participating in it.

Now Debbie is the main carer for her father. She doesn't find the practical things too difficult, but anything involving communication doesn't come easily. Communication makes her stressed very quickly.

People who knew Debbie's mum now visit her dad. But he says very little, so the responsibility for conversing falls on Debbie. Women are expected to be able to chat, but she has no idea what to talk about. She tries to act neurotypical and be all friendly and chatty. Over time, she's become good at 'small talk' and she feels reasonably comfortable as long as she knows it will only last for a limited time.

Something that helps her cope is being in touch with others who also care for their elderly parents. Just being able to talk to people who understand is great because Debbie doesn't feel so isolated.

Debbie says she still feels and acts much younger than her age:

> 'If I am talking to women in their 20s I feel I can laugh at silly things and if I can have a bit of a lark playing a game of ten-pin bowling with a group of 25-year-old Aspie girls then I feel so much better afterwards.'

This shows us that even when an older person with ASC has responsibilities and can relate quite well to others, they still may be much younger socially than their physical age.

It is more important than ever for Debbie's home to feel like a place of sanctuary. She needs to have things around her that make her feel calm and happy. In her flat she can be totally herself and not worry about others. When the doorbell or the telephone rings, she ignores it when she wants to. Email suits her just fine as it's not an intrusion into her peace and she can reply when she feels like it.

Debbie's pet budgies have really helped her to cope with life and getting older. She thinks pets keep you grounded when things get really difficult as they continue to chirp and sing no matter what. They give her a sense of normality at times when everything feels chaotic.

She loves being creative with her arts and crafts, too. It really helps lift her mind from worries. Maybe this works for Debbie because this is an area of interest – it's Debbie's passion.

Debbie enjoys sitting in coffee shops. She thinks that's her favourite thing to do and it makes her feel good. She likes the way it's okay nowadays for people to just sit in a coffee shop by themselves. Debbie says:

> 'There's something nice about feeling you're part of the world but not having the stress of having to communicate.'

Older people with ASC all relate to this, especially when communication is so taxing. We need to create quiet and safe spaces for our older people with ASC.

Debbie's story is a familiar one and the kind of story I hear often from many older ASC individuals, highlighting difficulties with slower processing, modified socialising and experiencing isolation. Debbie is fortunate in that she has found a way to live with her ageing and with her autism, mostly not allowing social demands to take over and sap her energy.

Summary

This chapter has expressed a variety of communication needs that govern being an older individual with ASC. It has shown though the literature and personal stories that different strategies work in different ways and for different individuals. Getting to know the older person with ASC, their strengths and interests, so these can be incorporated into all management plans, is primary to successful communication.

☞ Key points

- It is the right of all involved with the older person with ASC to be sharing the same information in ways that make sense to all.

- Some will be like Debbie, very able and very accepting of who they are and of their limitations. Others will need much more support and may or may not be able to convey their needs. So, finding communication strategies that work is essential (e.g. digital tablets, pen and paper, photographs, video).

- If the appropriate communication strategies are employed, the right information can be shared, acted upon, monitored and maintained.

CHAPTER 3

Working with Personality

Introduction

Communication issues and coping with change are also impacted by personality. This chapter explores the relationship between personality and processing style, and considers daily accessibility difficulties.

Personality types

It has been postulated that four particular personality types exist within a diagnosis of ASC (e.g. Wing 2000).[1] I'm not convinced it is as black and white as this, but this structure gives us a place to start. Personality types and social interaction styles are connected (e.g. Scheeren, Koot and Begeer 2012).

The four personality types impacting on social interaction styles are:

- *Aloof personality.* This group is thought of as the most common group in ASC. Individuals often act indifferently to those around them. They may show

---

1   See www.visualsupportsandbeyond.co.uk/why/triad.html and www.awares.org/static_docs/about_autism.asp?docSection=3.

little facial expression and might react to light touch but respond better to decisive and firm instructions.

- *Passive personality.* Some say this is the least common group. Females with ASC are more likely to be in this group. Just like the aloof group, people in the passive group may develop stress-related behaviour support needs but, when under pressure, are not able to connect with thoughts and feelings or verbalise the needs that arise from understanding thoughts and feelings the way NT individuals do.

- *Active but odd personality.* This group makes active approaches towards social contact but may have no real understanding of social rules. People in this group tend to be tactile, though sometimes do not judge the circumstances where propriety is needed.

- *Over-formal and stilted personality.* This group tries very hard to behave correctly and well, but may have no true understanding of social rules. Thus, people in this group tend to be very rigid with a need to obey rules they have learnt with no appreciation of times or occasions when it is okay to bend the rules or abandon them.[2]

Learning styles

As well as being particular personality types, individuals also have learning styles. In ASC this is vital to understand because often personality and learning styles are crowded out

---

2   For example, 'Bones' from the TV show: www.fox.com/bones.

by the autism and people forget this. The main four learning styles are:

- *Visual.* Learn best by seeing (e.g. pictures, video, posters, maps).

- *Kinaesthetic.* A special orientation and awareness. Learn best by doing (rather than watching a task, the best thing for this person is to map it out, pace it out and to do it themselves).

- *Auditory.* Learn best by listening (e.g. listening to a phone number and typing it into their phone rather than copying it from a written format).

- *Tactile.* Needs to feel their way around the environment. Kinaesthetic and tactile are highly correlated.

Of course, most individuals have a mix of learning styles and accommodating the dominant style is what is important. One person commented:

'I think the learning styles theme is a bit out of date. I think the emphasis now is providing learning experiences to all that they use multiple presentation/learning styles, rather than pigeonholing learners into one style.' (Anonymous, personal communication)

The above is true, but, at the same time we need to check in with older ASC individuals and find their areas of strength and of need. We each learn differently and there is no one size that fits all.

Personality changes

Just like in the general population, in the case of older people with ASC personality changes over time. However, how much depends upon certain factors, such as cooperating with a growing understanding of 'self' and the need to build social skills, and the individual's chosen response to these factors. Some suggest personality changes up to 5 per cent as individuals learn to adapt in their personas (Hooker and McAdams 2003).

Personality change reflects an ability to adapt. However, adaptation is difficult for those of us with ASC because we process information one sense at a time and not as a shared sensory experience. For example, we process hearing separately from seeing and separately from tasting – although, of course, when something is familiar to us these senses are already primed and will work together. The NT population can process several senses at any one time; this frees them to access the bigger picture more quickly and, in turn, to return communication as needed. By the time people with ASC are in a similar place, often the opportunity to communicate with someone has passed. Hence, conversations can be very uncomfortable.

Personality has been shown to predict the wellbeing response following important life events such as unemployment (Boyce, Wood and Brown 2010), disability (Boyce and Wood 2011b), widowhood (Pai and Carr 2010) and income changes (Boyce and Wood 2011a). I hope we are all learning and all changing for the better as time passes; but believing that one can contribute to one's life style in a positive manner contributes positively to a sense of wellbeing. In the ASC ageing population, however, perceived control over one's life may be less a factor in wellbeing than in the NT world.

This is because older people in the NT population have a bigger say in their life choices simply because they are aware of them and have the communication skills to negotiate them. In the ageing ASC population, however, where communication skills, social skills and an ability to work with personality style are less available, a sense of control over one's life is also lacking. This is not such an issue for the younger ASC population who have families to assist them and can work together over issues involving daily decisions.

Exploring ways to uncover and propagate a sense of control needs to begin internally for people with ASC. When someone has a sense of feeling good about themselves they can begin to take that internal sense and project it outwards. The particular personality style of the older ASC individual will impact how individuals perceive themselves and others (James *et al.* 2011). Understanding personality styles creates access for constructive communication when carers appreciate how and why the ASC individuals behave in certain ways.

Due to the nature of ASC, older people are pretty set in their ways with little space for coping with new things. But growing older often means having to deal with all manner of new things associated with diet, body, environment, health, energy and so on. These changes need to be managed and included in any management plan along with the individual's capacity to adapt. Communication style, personality style and learning styles all play a significant part in forming older ASC individuals' capacity for change.

As ASC individuals, our particular personality style impacts how we perceive and handle new information; this has many implications for communication. For example, older individuals with ASC may take verbal information quite literally (leading to difficulty with translation of metaphorical concepts), then filter it through their specific learning style (visual, auditory, tactile, kinaesthetic and various combinations of these), as well as their personality style (introvert, extrovert, socially keen, anxious, and so on). So, if you are a visual learner who happens to be 'aloof and odd' in your personality description, which means you are probably introverted and withdrawn, you might hear a metaphor such as, 'I can tell he feels hen pecked' (literal meaning: pecked by chickens; metaphorical meaning: is being verbally got at, bossed about and dictated to) and the meaning for you could be the visual one rather than the metaphorical one. It could mean you develop an unrealistic fear of female chickens! This analogy could be the case for all people, but being both ASC and older brings with it some particular challenges, mostly associated with being single-minded and literal thinkers, which are discussed throughout this book.

As well as personality and learning styles, interactions between staff and individuals also affect communication and understanding. If a person feels heard, valued and respected, they are more likely to respond in a positive manner. If they sense that the help on offer is not informed or there is little understanding of who they are as an older person with ASC, their cooperation may be less forthcoming.

An older NT individual may notice what is happening for their carers. They may try not to upset the people around them and/or hide discomforts if they think they could be building a reputation as someone who complains, or isn't grateful or appreciative. In ASC we rarely notice the mood of another, might not appreciate that our behaviour could be upsetting others and may have no interest in what others think of us. Interestingly, though, I have noticed that ASC individuals often notice authenticity (e.g. they pick up on whether individuals are doing a job because they have to rather than because they care about it).

How personality affects lifestyle changes

Some older ASC individuals are more open and welcoming of support than others. These individuals are not less ASC but are less suspicious and less anxious. But if an ASC individual chooses to be less social or doesn't respond to a family or team member then it is more than likely a personality trait rather than a personal rebuff to the kindly support offered by others. Understanding people and their personalities will mean that carers can better support ASC individuals.

If an individual seems aloof...

Aloof older people with ASC may be highly embarrassed easily. This means that they avoid the limelight and anything that increases personal anxiety. Being tactile avoidant yet still needing human affirmation is a dilemma not easily understood by the person themselves or those caring for them. It becomes difficult to do simple things, such as answer to one's name or answer the doorbell. Answering the telephone is an incredibly uncomfortable action and yet failing to do so can cause others to see them as rude, or cause them to miss vital information.

To assist with keeping others at bay, aloof individuals may give an air of distance or seem uninterested. The older ASC individual may prefer to stay in their own room or find another space of their own, and will not like shared dining or other arranged group events. They are not being anti-social but are trying to cope in the best way they know how. Even so, these behaviours can offend people supporting them.

Such individuals need set rules and structure as well as pre-warning of routine changes. Communication must be black and white with no grey areas. Situations in which others have changed their mind or have changed their expectations for the individual concerned can be experienced as disappointment or even seen as dishonest.

An individual with an aloof style will not seek friendship and will appear not to care. Being intolerant of others leads some people to think of such older people with ASC as anti-social, but mostly this behaviour is born out of a desire to cope. At the same time, ASC individuals from the aloof group can be open to abuse due to naivety. If other people are critical, judgemental, sarcastic or rude, the individual at whom this is directed is unlikely to recognise it. That is, they find it difficult to separate teasing in fun from actual emotional abuse.

It is common for aloof individuals to not cope with social, physical or emotional expectations due to these being experienced as demands. But, not being able to verbalise this, older ASC individuals might need to use 'behaviour' to make their point. It can be hard to communicate needs, likes and dislikes to family and care staff. Such individuals may go along to outings and share times with others for a season, then will have meltdowns (physical, emotional or/and social collapse) when things get overwhelming. This happens because when senses are full there just isn't space for any more processing.

If an individual seems passive...

A passive older person with ASC appears to have no mind of their own. They fit in and do whatever is suggested. This may mean going along with the group (in spite of possibly not wanting to) and may also mean being easily overwhelmed. Staff can see this when the individual has sudden eruptions of behaviour that seem to come from nowhere. The person may have no expression on their face that indicates what they are experiencing, so it is difficult to read them (Kleinhans *et al.*

2008). They may have a monotone voice, will say yes but mean no, and will not complain. Still, they resent decisions that don't go their way.

Those in this personality group also need set rules and structure in their daily lives. They will need notice and pre-warning of routine changes rather than surprises. Thinking and processing styles will be black and white, and there will be no hint that they don't understand the grey areas. If others change their mind about expectations and events for them, the individual will feel lied to and let down. As they see it, they were given the daily newsletter with all events outlined. This was their timetable, their diary, for what to expect. If this changes without consultation it is as if they have been misled.

Such individuals will not seek friendship and will appear not to care either way. They may appear tolerant but be building up resentment, not equipped with how to express feelings. This leaves them open to abuse due to their not recognising or noticing critical or judgemental dispositions of others, including support staff. Like the aloof group, the passive group can easily be taken for granted by others but won't recognise this. Going along with outings and activities may lead to meltdowns that seem to come out of the blue.

If an individual seems active, but odd...

Those in this group of older people with ASC appear to want to join in with others but will only do so if plans go their way or they feel in control. Many will not recognise the ideas and plans of others as being important, due to only seeing things from their perspective. Appearing eccentric, self-centred, controlling and dominant on the one hand, they still need to be involved in activities.

Being driven to be on the move, those in this group need action and have difficulty being still. Therefore they will need projects and purpose. They also need set rules and structure delivered through previously negotiated guidelines detailing how they like things done. The active-but-odd individuals also need pre-warning of routine changes and to be in agreement with those changes. Their processing style will be black and white with no tolerance of grey areas. They will seek friendship but on their terms, appearing bossy and dominant.

These older people appear to care, but only as long as things go their way. This is not a disposition towards selfishness; it is just that they don't recognise 'other', unless the other's portrait is painted and communicated in the way that makes sense to them, or in a way that they relate to.

I remember a psychiatrist asking me how I would feel if my partner died. I replied it would depend on the day and what I was expecting. For example, if it was a Friday (a day that we went to McDonald's for breakfast) I would feel worried because my partner takes me out for breakfast. If she wasn't able to, then who would take me to McDonald's? This remark seems callous and uncaring, but it simply shows how my mind is taken up with routines and my need to stay within them. I cannot forward-think easily so it is difficult to know what might happen when a routine is interrupted. This is not being cold and insensitive. If the psychiatrist had worded the question differently, for example: 'When your partner dies will you be sad?' my reply would have been, 'I will be incredibly sad.'

Just like with other personality styles, not being tolerant of others is one side of the coin but the other is not noticing when they are being abused. These older people are open to abuse due to not recognising or noticing critical or judgemental dispositions. This means they put up with being taken for granted by others but will not identify such or be able to let family and care staff know their needs, dislikes and preferred ways of going about things. Many older people with this disposition will enjoy outings, socialising and sharing with others, but in an odd way (e.g. may be too loud, too close, inappropriate) and will have meltdowns when overwhelmed.

If an individual seems over-formal and stilted...

This group may come across as not caring about fashion, preferring to wear their own familiar clothing. Even if clothing is not appropriate to the season or time of year, the setting, age or occasion, they may insist that they wear the clothes they are used to. This group of older people with ASC need set rules for everything, including dinner wear, place settings, personal hygiene and belongings, leisure activities, and who does what with whom, when, where, how often, and so on.

Many with this personality write everything down in triplicate and check off happenings accordingly. Not being able to tolerate changes to routines, they will insist that everything goes according to their expectations and timetable. Operating with clockwork dependability is usual for the stilted, formal group and they will expect the same from others.

All set rules and structured outlines must be obeyed. Any change to expectations requires early and carefully communicated notice. Their understandings will be black and white with no tolerance of grey areas. When others have a change of mind, or change their expectations of a timetabled event, older people with ASC from the stilted, formal group will be very stressed and upset. Behaviour (e.g. vocally too loud, possibly aggressive, insistence on doing things their way or not at all) will clearly demonstrate this.

When it comes to socialising they might seek friendship but will do so in an over-zealous way. This means possibly forming an over-attachment to a preferred other with no sense of that person's wellbeing. Living their lives through another person might be their only way to access understanding of everyday things. It's as if the other person becomes their eyes, ears and legs.

This personality disposition leads an individual to be less tolerant, but at the same time they are open to abuse due to not noticing or recognising critical or judgemental dispositions of others. Putting up with being taken for granted by others while at the same time displaying a 'bossy', domineering disposition makes them difficult to understand.

These individuals are not good at conveying their needs and likes to family and care staff. They might enjoy outings and sharing with others, but in an odd and formal way with everything being explained and nothing deviating from expectations. If there is a deviation, many will have meltdowns due to being overwhelmed.

★ ★ ★

The ageing ASC individual will need teaching, training and care according to their personality and learning styles. As well, all of the processes of ageing require appropriate communication, but using words alone, as one might, does not aid processing information as it does in NT aged care.

Digital communication tools, such as iPads, iPhones, personal PCs and so on, help older people with ASC not to get hung up on body language, facial expression or tone of voice. These tools allow them to go straight to the point in all areas of life. In many countries around the world, these older individuals are being given the chance to learn how to use the internet. Technology offers a wealth of information, online shopping opportunities, health advice and so on that are easier to navigate because they don't have body-language or facial expressions to decode first. Social media (e.g. Facebook) enables those with ASC who are elderly to accommodate many of their needs for social contact.

Helpful technology software on tablets and computers includes accessible functions such as changing font size, background colour, text to speech, and so on, making an ordinary personal computer a brilliant communication tool for older people with ASC. For example, Dragon software that converts voice to text is useful for those who may find conversation difficult, have vision issues and need time to process sentences. There are applications (apps) for computers and tablets and a book called *Apps for Autism* (Brady 2011), which gives an idea of which apps work best and what they do. Due to these being constantly updated I have not included a list here, but encourage you to check out what is currently available by typing 'Apps and Autism' into your computer's search engine. Suffice it to say that communication via a digital device accommodates all personality styles and learning styles whether a person is a visual learner who is introverted or an auditory learner who is extroverted.

Management plan

Once carers know and understand an individual's personality and learning style, a management plan that considers their needs can be explored, developed and refined. Such a management plan may consist of the following:

- Listing individual goals.

- Sorting, prioritising and budgeting for goals.

- Breaking down the activity into manageable bites of date, time and length of activity.

- Noting all events directly before and after.

- Constructing, implementing, monitoring and evaluating timetables.

Summary

This chapter has explored the idea that personality and learning styles, although not set and likely to change over time, do have an influence on how older people with ASC relate, communicate, understand themselves and others as well as contribute to knowing the best way for information to be offered and received. Technology accommodates all learning styles and can be constructively interactive.

⚑ Key points

- Each older person with ASC is an individual. Sometimes their physical age will not match their emotional and/ or social age.

- Those working with and supporting older people with ASC need to understand personality style and learning style(s). This essential component will aid all communication between carers, family and the older people. No one personality suits all learning styles and vice-versa.

- Personality style and learning style impacts choices, decision-making, personal relationships and goal completion.

- All activities, plans and programmes need to be person-centred.

- Ideas must be managed according to the above. These must also be implemented, updated, maintained and advanced according to changing information.

CHAPTER 4

Identifying Feelings, Thoughts and Actions

Introduction

Chapters 1 to 3 explored communication and personality in older people with ASC. But the premise for all communication is that an individual has an understanding of what it is to communicate. For neurotypical (NT) individuals, expressions of joy, excitement, discomfort, anger and so on can be communicated well. The social understanding about timing, propriety, and how and when to express feelings and thoughts is part of being typical. However, as we have seen, this is not part of being autistic. Connecting to and communicating with one's joys and needs is difficult due to the lack of social skills, yes, but also due to not having the understanding of them in the first place.

Some older people with ASC will appreciate what and where their discomfort or happiness springs from, but many of these ASC individuals may not. When you are living a life that is cognitively challenging, possibly with many sensory issues, you may be switched off from names and connections to things. You may know you are uncomfortable or comfortable. You may know something has changed but be unsure of what that is. You may not have the words, feelings or appropriate actions to express yourself, but are being driven to 'act' in some way to communicate this.

When an individual is living with these discomforts they might use 'behaviour' to tell you. The behaviour easily misleads if you take a typical view. For example, the behaviour might seem aggressive, jealous, selfish or monotonous. These are often called 'challenging' behaviours but, as mentioned earlier in this book, actually they are 'stress support behaviours' (or needs) that indicate that an individual is stressed and needs help. Stress support needs particularly occur when individuals have not been shown (or are not confident in) any alternative way to communicate their needs.

Changing terminology, but are we changing attitudes?

As well as building concepts that create understanding for older people with ASC themselves, we need to challenge the attitudes of those who support them. We can change the terminology as much as we like, but if attitudes don't change then the terms used are empty and shallow. For example, if we call the behaviour 'stress support needs' but carers still *think* 'challenging behaviours', they miss the point of the change in terminology. When thinking 'this behaviour is challenging us' we are looking at the individual's behaviour as being 'their problem'. Consequently, we need to teach them to behave better. This misses the point of why the behaviour is there (i.e. to call for help).

Understanding that this behaviour is the result of stress and difficulties with communication means that the individual needs support to help reduce stress levels. Only then can we learn to understand one another because the carer gets to know the real reason for the behaviour and see the older person with ASC behind the behaviour (not the person acting out under stress). Looking beyond the behaviour enables the carer to put measures into place that support the individual and stress them less. All management plans need to consider the possibility that stress is behind 'behaviours'.

Stressors

When NT individuals are told to expect something and then it doesn't happen, they might feel disappointed or frustrated. But with having a word for the feeling and the capacity to reason, they can arrive at a point of resolution through contemplating the possibilities of why this has happened. If, however, you are an older person with ASC and no one has helped you understand, it can seem like you are upset over nothing. I was well into my forties before I realised that people were allowed to change their minds. I knew they changed their minds, I had experienced this. But I didn't know it was allowed!

What happened was that a fellow student studying with me (I went to university as a mature student) had been taking a few of us in her car to McDonald's between lectures, on a Tuesday. McDonald's was one of my favourite fast food outlets and I loved to go there. Being very single-minded, however, I started anticipating and thinking about the visit to McDonald's and couldn't focus on the lecture.

On one occasion when I asked if we were going to 'MaCers' she said, 'Not today, Wenn. It's Susie's birthday so I have to buy her a card; I have to go to the Post Office and do some other things too.' I was furious! It seemed to me that just when I was beginning to trust this person and think of her as 'my friend', she was taking my 'joy' away.

I couldn't stay at uni that day. When I got home I phoned the man I had seen during some assessments I'd had. He said, 'Wenn, people are allowed to change their minds.' For me this was a light-bulb moment. It was the word 'allowed' that made all the difference. Lots of things had happened to me over the years that made me sad, angry, happy and so on. But I often didn't know what the emotion was for, why it was there or what it meant. On this occasion I learnt about all three.

When something goes wrong (e.g. the unexpected happens), typical individuals will usually talk about it and have little trouble explaining to others. Using words to try to explain things is not a problem for most people. But what if you didn't understand verbal information because you weren't given enough time to process it, you were not connected to the information, it was too abstract and so on? This might be the life for many older people with ASC. This is different from what is happening in children with ASC due to the nature of the differences experienced in older adult life (e.g. possible loss of bladder control; more aches and pains; less need for sleep). So, what if you couldn't 'feel' your bodily functions and didn't have, for example:

- words to explain feelings

- connection to appetite

- awareness of public and private

- bladder and bowel connection to urgency

- feelings of tiredness connecting to sleepiness and wakefulness

- typical timing of auditory processes (e.g. length of pauses in conversation, taking turns to speak, etc.).

Without the right understanding, connections and tools, what might you do instead of using speech to communicate? You might use behaviour (e.g. shouting, biting, pushing, flapping, humming, thumping, spitting)!

Sound, speech, ageing and decoding

According to Mayer and Heaton (2014), both sensory abnormalities and ageing impact on speech encoding in ASC. For example, when someone is talking to older autistic individuals the sounds they use may travel to the brain in the usual way but our senses can distort them *en route*. The encoding that should occur to enable us to understand the sounds as 'speech' and work out the meaning will be disrupted. This makes it very difficult to understand speech when it is delivered at speed, or in a metaphorical manner, or if other background noises and activities are co-existing.

How often does this occur? For typical older people hearing is a strain, but for older people with ASC it is not just difficult to hear the words, it is difficult to attach meaningful understanding.

The solution is not to speak to them so slowly that they feel like idiots. Their understanding will improve if carers and supporters:

- speak clearly

- avoid metaphor

- speak when no other noises are competing for attention

- speak when the older person's attention is not otherwise occupied

- say what you mean and mean what you say.

Obsessions or passions?

The *DSM-5* criteria for a positive assessment of ASC point out 'repetitive interests'. Some of our gifts and strengths can be found in the activities and abilities that interest us. These can be single-focused and thought of as 'repetitive'. Yet often they're an asset, not a hindrance. For example, if we know that an individual loves to shop (i.e. this is a particular interest for them) we could help them construct a catalogue of 'goodies' and 'reject items'. We can extrapolate the love of shopping into the ASC individual's broader world. Goodies and rejects can represent wants, desires or dislikes. No words are necessary for this. For example, by using an appropriate catalogue of pictures that represent 'happy' and 'unhappy' for an individual, such as food they love to eat whilst out and food they dislike, we can help to build concepts associated with happy, unhappy, like and dislike. *Note:* Remember the role of gamma, which is triggered during motivation; interests are motivating and lead to strengths that are empowering and enable communication.

The idea is to help the older person with ASC to build connections to things they feel, need, hope for, and so on. This necessitates the creating of concepts and the processing that accompanies being an individual or part of a group. Concepts (e.g. time, possession, public, private, now, later, happy, sad) exist as platforms to give access to communication. The concepts of everyday life may be emotive, factual, informative, creative, mundane, trivial or life-changing. But, if an individual has no place for such concepts or if they are so black and white in their thinking they can't relate to the necessary 'greys' they need to, it makes communication very difficult. Reasoning isn't reasonable if we cannot connect to reason because we don't have the concepts. These need to be built up and established first before connection and communication with oneself and others are possible.

Gender

It is widely believed that many more females exist who would qualify for a diagnosis of ASC than previously thought. Also there seem to be more females being diagnosed later in life. Life events that may lead to women seeking a diagnosis include relationship breakdown, loss of career or meeting individuals who offer support that previously wasn't available to them. Opportunities for diagnosis are occurring more for older individuals than they were in the past (Carol Povey of the NAS Ageing Project 2014, personal communication). However, most of the literature on ASC only deals with males on the autism spectrum.

When we look at the gender ratio of older individuals with autism across the world, traditionally males outweigh females as a general rule. However, in reality the numbers are pretty equal, especially when intelligence quotient (IQ) and developmental quotient (DQ)[1] are factored in (Fombonne 2003; Worley and Matson 2011). This means that when we remove some of the obstacles related to IQ and DQ, the

1   Developmental quotient refers to a numerical measure of an infant's performance on a developmental schedule relative to the performance of other infants of the same age.

gender ratio diminishes and male and female numbers look more alike with regard to their autism than they otherwise appear. This is not the same as saying that male and female ASC individuals are all the same. We know this isn't true (Lai *et al.* 2011).

Generally we think of women as being more socially inclined than men. This also appears to be true for individuals with ASC, but only for the more cognitively able (higher functioning). In the general population we know that females live longer. What will this mean for autistic women as they age? As far as I know there isn't any research that talks to this. It stands to reason that if you are cognitively challenged *and* have other health issues, life will throw up extra trials so you will need more support as you get older with all manner of daily activities.

No matter what their gender, people need to feel in control of their own lives. There is, in general, a greater demand upon women and the roles they play. Women, more than men, are expected to be more social, more 'connected' to the emotions of self and of other and more 'in touch' generally. Men are forgiven more. Whatever your gender though, feeling like you have some say in your life can make a whole heap of difference to your mood, outlook and expectation in life. So, imagine how you might feel if someone else dictated your daily activities all the way from selecting your clothing to your television programmes? This is exactly what happens for so many older individuals with ASC, seven days a week, 365 days a year. Yet, once concepts are established and individuals have connections to the understanding they need, software programs such as those produced by www.spectronics. com.au (e.g. non-text-based email) can give the means for individuals, even those who might not read and write, to share with others what it is that they think, feel and need.

Software that uses pictures (those with the software and the individual's own photographs), for example, to put together information that others can 'read', can inform all concerned and keep us on the same page. This is explained in more detail in 'Communication: Assistive technology' in Chapter 7.

I know I have trouble identifying some of the emotive states I travel through. In ASC, at whatever age, the basis for repetitive and stereotyped interests has been related to difficulties with shifting attention. This is one major reason why engaging in social conversation, and other activity (e.g. recognising feelings), is so difficult for us as individuals with ASC. For example, to engage socially depends upon being able to attend (note) the physical, cognitive, emotional and sensory aspects of 'self' and of 'other' (Frith and Happé 1999). Therefore, one needs access or an attention window to each of these. But being governed by narrow motivation (repetitive interests) means only being able to attend to one aspect of these, if interested, not all simultaneously.

Why is this important for us as ageing ASC individuals? It is important because people expect us to look at them when they talk to us. It is important because those supporting us as we age expect us to notice them, to hear them and respond quickly to their questions. Children and younger people with ASC are often excused due to their younger age, but older individuals with ASC are not afforded this same leniency.

Some differences between older females and older males with ASC

- For older women on the autism spectrum, special interests are often not seen as special because they may be commonly found in the general population of women. The difference is that their interests dominate over all else. This can hinder them from being able to switch interests easily.

• Females with ASC are often said to lack empathy but, actually, I find they are often over-empathetic, which means that they turn away from situations that require their attention. For example, when a person is sick or needy the autistic older woman may not be able to cope with that person's demand. Not because they don't care, but because their discomfort overwhelms them.

• Sometimes ASC women's love of animals, music, art, literature and even fashion or certain people can overtake them in ways that cause them to obsess. Men are equally passionate about the things that interest them but they are more prone to interests in science, numbers, maps, video games, strategy games, engineering and politics. Of course women may share these passions, too. Why is this important to know? It is important because as older ASC individuals our passions may stay stuck in time; they might not age with us.

• Older females with ASC might need lots of support and it is expected that they will share their concerns with others, as women tend to do so more than men. But they find it difficult to identify needs, let alone explain them to or explore them with others. Males on the spectrum, however, tend to be more rigid, less social and even less emotional than females. This is also seen in the typical population, but carers and other supporters of ASC individuals need to check in with the men and tell them, rather than ask them, what their needs are. It is a gender difference that easily transfers to the ASC population but is not one that we necessarily recognise, experience or appreciate. Therefore, we may fail to accommodate it.

- Like NT females, ageing females with autism go through a number of hormonal changes that affect their body temperature, appetite and ability to cope with change. According to research, these changes may be perceived in greater depth and experience when compared to the same hormone changes in NT females. This is because of the sensory disposition to 'notice more' in ASC. The single minded focus also allows ASC individuals to ruminate and fixate more obsessively, making the whole experience stronger and more overwhelming (Lawson 2011). If those who support them are unaware of these things and if the individuals themselves cannot tell you, then obsessional behaviour or stress support needs will result. It is very important, therefore, that people supporting these individuals can check in with them concerning these issues. Just because individuals might not talk doesn't mean they don't think. Nor does it mean that they cannot communicate their needs to another. But it does mean that those working with them need to get to know them individually and find appropriate communication devices.

- Older autistic individuals may be totally unaware of the age differences that exist between them and others. I know I find it very difficult to tell another individual's age and this can mean I'm insecure about how to relate to them. While this is true for both genders, in men the resultant behaviour can have serious and upsetting consequences (e.g. inappropriate sexual activity, stalking).

- Older individuals with ASC may have some unusual sensory processing issues. This is also seen within the NT population but, when added to our obsessive or passionate dispositions in ASC, we can develop tantrum behaviours that may not be seen in our younger selves. Due to their greater strength, this behaviour can cause more concern in older males.

- Younger women with ASC may get very anxious, just like males with ASC; however, females' anxiety is rarely physical or disruptive in their younger years. Such individuals often turn their anxiety inwards to depression and paranoia. It's as if it just isn't 'ladylike' to tantrum! Not having legitimate expression for their anxiety builds up over time and, during menopause in particular, their walls crumble and they can often no longer hold it together.

- Older ASC females who may once have been described as shy, quiet, solitary or loners will find it very difficult coming to terms with the changes they are experiencing as their physical bodies age. This is true for most women, whether typical or autistic. But, if you are a member of the NT population, you have access to a variety of materials to help you through this transition. Also, you may not live with sensory dysphoria and the battle to understand what is happening to you will be easier.

- Males with ASC don't go through menopause, but they may face physical differences that impact upon sexual libido, muscle tone and loss of head and body hair. These changes can be suddenly noticed rather than grow slowly with the individual. Such shock can cause panic and, therefore, the individual will have a variety of behaviour support needs. But trying to explain these won't be easy because the individuals themselves may not realise what is happening to them. This is another reason why older people with ASC need people to get to know and anticipate their needs. It's also a reason why giving them the appropriate means to build concepts to assist them to communicate is so important.

The above are generalisations and one must not assume they are always the case for every person. Therefore we must respect and learn about each situation and get to know each individual for who they are.

Many other noticeable differences between the genders are just that: gender issues. Some individuals like feminine pursuits while others, even though they are female, may be inclined to less feminine activities. It's the same for the men. Being male does not always mean you will like beer and footy! Whatever your gender, you are an individual and will need others in your life to take the time to get to know you.

Brain scan technology

Brain scan technology is allowing us to discover more and more about which part of our brain does what and why. For example, advances in brain scanning technology are making it easier to understand the ways in which brains are 'wired' differently.

Already some research indicates that brain scans can identify ASC (Duffy and Als 2012) and can show us the areas of the brain implicated (Ecker *et al.* 2011), thus directing us to appropriate interventions and support. However, due to the costs and availability of equipment such scans are rarely accessible. What they do teach us is there are reasons for the behaviour we see in ASC and why this is changing for individuals as they age.

Strengths in ASC and in ageing

Current patterns being shown by brain imaging technology in individuals with autism are indicating that there are reasons for exploring autistic strengths rather than just weaknesses (e.g. Dawson *et al.* 2007; Schneider 2011).

In society, usefulness is highly valued. If we are seen as having value, we are more likely to feel good about ourselves; more likely to have confidence in those supporting us; and more likely to age with dignity and respect, rather than with paranoia, self-harm and neglect. If older people with ASC can demonstrate usefulness, those around them are likely to be more accepting of their social ineptness and more accommodating of the difficulties they live with.

Social skills

As people with ASC age, their social skills don't automatically improve. They don't learn as regular individuals do. They do learn, but they learn differently. Understanding this can help them to apply the right technologies in their chosen interventions so they can learn those skills and techniques necessary to enable them to function better in life. Digital tablets, for example, can be the 'seeing-eye dog' for older people with ASC because they can give a voice to help them communicate with others, via pictures or text, and enable them to develop texting and keyboard skills that allow them to type when speech is too difficult to utilise or is unavailable.

Emphasising strengths

It is important to remember that older people with ASC are very good at many things, especially anything requiring structure, format, attention to detail, order and sameness. However, for many, ordinary everyday change can be very uncomfortable. I think this is because:

- As ageing ASC individuals we are designed to be good with one thing at any one time. However, this means we are not good at thinking, doing or being more than one thing at one time. For example, we look *or* listen; we focus on detail *not* the whole picture.

- Therefore we find it hard to predict consequences. We don't easily appreciate probabilities or note clues that lead to forming an appropriate conclusion. So, how will we recognise matters as being urgent, emergencies or priorities? It's hard to tell the difference.

- We tend to think in closed frames (pictures, scenarios, concepts) and, because each is different, we find it hard to generalise. This is limiting, for example, because if you can't prioritise or recognise urgent from important but not urgent, there is extra stress. Individuals are more at risk of making mistakes and/or of not taking things seriously that need to be taken seriously. For example, I always feel the urge to answer the telephone when it rings. Sometimes it's not convenient, though, because I might be cooking tea or attending to some other need. But if the phone rings I have been known to leave the stove to answer the phone and then almost burn the house down because the fat in the fry pan caught alight. My daughter helped me learn to let the answering machine take the calls and I've learnt to call people back, if they ask me to.

Some autistic people have made scientific advances that have changed the lives of thousands. For example, Temple Grandin, a woman now in her sixties, diagnosed with autism as a young child, is well known for her animal husbandry skills and specific design of cattle chutes; she has a worldwide reputation for her work with cattle in that domain and with animals in general. In Schneider's (2011) experiments using neuro-feedback from fibre tracking of the brain's circuits with Grandin, he found that her brain shows dramatic disorganisation of the part used in language. Even so, Grandin, with her lack of social prowess, is a very successful businesswoman who has set plans in motion to take care of herself in her elderly seasons of life. For example, she has appropriate health and life insurance as well as appointed carers to help her with domestic duties and her paperwork (personal communication 2012).

Management and evaluation plan

From the above, if you think about life from the perspective of an older person with ASC you can imagine why change can be so difficult. Change isn't easy for older people generally, but society usually accommodates this and provides strategies to help them to cope. For older people with ASC, any provisions need to consider what is known about ageing and about ASC. I think the following could be useful for those of us with ASC:

- Collaborate with us to **design a system** that works for both the individual and the carer. For example, colour coding, numbering, naming and/or sorting by some means according to types, products, placing, belongings, time of day. Having a system for a variety of projects is very useful. This will let us know where something fits and will assist us in knowing where to place displaced items. It also decreases panic and stress when we are confronted with change. At my home the only thing I need to remember if I come across displaced files, for example, is to place them into the inbox and my family will put them away. This helps to reduce my anxiety about items not being in their proper place.

- Tell us **social stories** that use intent, context and scale. Stories that explain social concepts are not just for children. As older people we often miss social concepts and so find it hard to read others. Helping us to plan for everyday events can assist us in knowing what to do, what to expect and when to expect it.

- What might this look like? We need others to explain the **rules and processes** that are used in our home or in the dwellings of others. They may use stories, maps, plans and so on to do this. We will not usually automatically know these things. Even if we know the rule for one event it doesn't necessarily mean we will know it for another, however similar.

- Using photos or other **visual cues** may be helpful. We tend to understand better when we can see the process. Digital video is great too. I can watch, stop the video, go back over things and watch it as many times as I need to. It's very reassuring.

- **Avoid changing things** without letting us know about it. Sudden change is very threatening and we may react with disappointment and even aggression. We feel violated. If you cannot prepare us in advance (sometimes just a few minutes in advance is enough time but for others the plans need to be slotted in well ahead of time) then social stories about 'unexpected change' are helpful. Having a distractor (e.g. food, particular interest) can also be useful, but may be more effective if it is only offered when sudden change occurs. For example, although 'special interests' are used all the time, one aspect of this can be kept and used only when 'changes' occur. This will help the individual to view change differently, and they may even associate change with good things.

As an ageing individual with ASC I depend upon other family members and close friends to interpret a variety of situations for me. This is also true of younger ASC individuals, but as we age our reasons for needing others in our life may change. I won't need help with my homework, with joining other children's games or with eating a meal, perhaps, but I will need support with a variety of group activities (according to my personality type), planning my day or sorting out my paperwork. I often wonder how it might be should my friends and family not be around. As I age, so do the rest of my family. If they should succumb to ill-health, or not be as able as I need them to be, what will happen to me? I know there are official respite places in my local community home for the aged, but will the staff appreciate my autism and understand me and my needs? Will they have the kind of structure I need and will I be safe there?

In autism we need structure

It is important to create visual prompts and icons to help ageing ASC individuals who may not use spoken language. These prompts and icons give us structure and routine. Starting a day a certain way will suggest that this is the way each and every day must start. So, structuring the work routine, and times at home or away in respite or the aged care facility, must consider the timescale, the activities and expected changes that will occur.

Language considerations

ASC individuals are very literal thinkers and will take what is said to them literally too. It is better for us if the people around us say what they mean and mean what they say. For example, it's better to say, 'I'll be there *around* nine o'clock in the morning to help you with the shopping' than to say, 'I'll be there *at* nine o'clock to help you with the shopping.' This small difference in the way time is presented makes such a big difference to older individuals with ASC. If you say nine o'clock but you turn up ten minutes later, then I might not let you in because you have missed your time.

Are family always better equipped to help?

Autism is most likely the result of genetics. This being so, we need to remember that ASC individuals are born into families where parents and siblings may be somewhere on the autistic spectrum themselves or have their own ASC edges. They may often have similar needs to those of the individual they are caring for.

For example, they may not have good organisational skills, not be good at thinking ahead and not have the kind of energy levels that NT family members have. This is because caring and supporting older people with ASC takes more out of the family than caring for non-autistic older people. Therefore, the family will need support that is practical, not just informational. This means, for example, they need help setting up the plans for routine schedules, not just being told that routine schedules are necessary, and having others assist with finding the materials to use.

Summary

The ageing brain in ASC shows the need to take spoken language more slowly than with NT individuals. Older people with ASC do learn. They might not find words to be the best resource for explaining their needs, but it is important to recognise their stress support needs and accommodate them appropriately. A **management and evaluation** plan will need to include time to look at behaviours and time to work out what is behind them.

Appreciating that older people with ASC are not children and will have lots of skills from their lifetime of learning is vital to building concepts and understanding. Learning to connect to our own thoughts, feelings, needs and wants is the basis for all communication. Finding appropriate interests, structures and ways to build meaning is easier once you understand how to connect with older people with ASC. Maintaining these supports is vitally important.

⚑ Key points

- Not having the words to express oneself is due in part to not having the concepts.

- Challenging behaviour ('acting out') should be thought of as 'stress support needs'. The problem is not in the behaviour but the stress behind it.

- Build social understanding so individuals have the foundation for communication. This needs to happen prior to the actual communication skills training.

- Please remember that ASC is genetic and families will need support to enable them to support their ASC member.

CHAPTER 5

Support for Older People in Transition

Introduction

As we know, ASC's impact on individuals varies according to age, gender, intellectual capacity and so on. Individuals can be very high-functioning (excuse the term; it reminds me of a piece of machinery, rather than a person) or live with cognitive delays and learning disability (lower functioning). Where an individual sits on the spectrum will impact how they cope with transition. Living with ASC isn't a static position; each person moves along and across the autism spectrum throughout a lifetime. Having appreciated that older people with ASC can develop concepts and connection to understanding via a variety of means (e.g. using interests, building connections, placing structures and routines into daily living) we then need to put action plans into operation. But we need to consider where an individual is on the spectrum at that time and what their individual transition needs are.

Therefore, to assist older people with ASC to transition through life, it is useful to understand what the individual might be looking forward to. To understand what is possible and any likely barriers. What of low-functioning individuals who are classically autistic – how do we specifically address their needs? What of risk assessment and how to assess this? The answers to these questions will guide the delivery of the required expertise for older people with ASC, wherever they are on the autism spectrum.

What are the individual's hopes, dreams and expectations?

It might be that the individuals we are supporting need help to build a retirement plan before leaving work. They may need help with choosing clothes or buying food on a daily basis. They may need support with adapting to the different seasons of the year, types of care support and carers, leisure options or changes within the family as elderly members die, and so much more. The individual might be facing the ultimate transition: the fact that they can no longer care for themselves and must move into aged care.

Some may experience a step back in time as they move from not knowing the reasons for their lifetime of unique difficulties to gaining a label that says they are autistic. Others, who were diagnosed as young children, will have never known any different.

However, late diagnosis of ASC is becoming more common. In this situation an individual has to rethink all they have known. For example, maybe they believed their difference from others was due to being intelligent. This may have led them into academia or some business venture. When socially they didn't 'fit' they blamed others for their ignorance. What happens to such individuals when work in their area ceases due to ageing? When everything they try falls through their fingers like sand? What happens when the institutions they have known don't want them any more, and various others (e.g. social clubs) are not places they relate to? These life transitions can trigger deeper ASC expression (e.g. rigid behaviours, obsessions, withdrawal), depression and further isolation.

I exist

I'm told that I exist because I am.
I'm told that I exist because I can.
So, if I'm not and cannot be
All that you have asked of me,
Do I still exist or will I cease to be?

Knowing what you hope for and actually living the reality of those hopes are two different things. I often need support to do the simplest of activities (e.g. ride on public transport; visit local shops; take care of bills and finances). However, I love to travel and visit foreign places. My hopes and dreams centre around foreign travel and the accompanying adventures. I find it difficult to imagine a future where I stay home and cannot fly overseas. But, the reality is that there will be a time when travel overseas is out of reach for me. In the meantime, though, I can still dream of exotic places.

Learning to separate one's dreams from one's everyday life is important but not always easy. All too often dreams and reality become muddled for people with ASC. By focusing on possibilities and creating an environment that is positive, plausible and welcoming, we can establish a life we are excited about.

Risk assessment

It is all too easy to decide that there are too many risks involved so it's best to do nothing. The biggest risk with this misguided thinking is that the person sinks into depression and gives up on life. It is much better to calculate and account for the risks, build safety nets where needed and encourage older people with ASC to have a go.

Risk assessment in a person with ASC is no different to risk assessment for other people. This means that as well as considering the risks in general we also need to identify the risks for the specific individual. For older people with ASC we should consider age, identified gender and physical limitations; available funding and human resources; individual interests, goals and possible outcomes; any given agency policy; cultural and social backgrounds; and, of course, the skills of the individual and the supporting team. Once having completed our assessments, we can identify the risks in specific areas and cater for them. This is a better option than closing the door on an individual's dreams simply because they seem too risky! Once goals and associated risks are identified, a management plan can be activated, implemented, monitored and evaluated, preferably with the involvement of the individuals themselves who are central to all planning.

Late diagnosis of ASC

Throughout the years I have encountered older individuals who have received an assessment of ASC in their later years. (I did not receive my current diagnosis until I was 42.) Although most of us are relieved we now have an explanation for the difficulties we have been living with, we are also often frustrated that it has taken so long and are full of regret that the same difficulties have cost us broken relationships and lost employment options. Some of us are estranged from our families and many feel a sense of having been let down by the system.

Paul says:

'…at last I have a diagnosis or assessment that tells me who I really am. But what does this mean now and where do I go next?'

Paul is asking an ordinary question and he needs an answer. But at times it is difficult to find an answer because it depends upon Paul's circumstances, support levels, available funding and access to the right connections. Most of us take it for granted that the resources we need in our later years will be available. However, this isn't always the case. For some, if you are an autistic older person and have an intellectual disability with an IQ below 70 you are considered low-functioning. This means you qualify for lots of adult services. You are probably in 'the system' and have received established care support over many years. This won't be the case though if you are of average IQ or above, have been employed and managed your life for several years in an accepted way.

Now that diagnostic criteria in the *DSM-5* allow for a diagnosis of autism in adulthood, gaining a late assessment will mean increased understanding for many who have lived socially confusing and frustrated lives. It also increases the number of older adults diagnosed with ASC, while not necessarily increasing provision or support for them.

In adult life ASC is diagnosed once daily life demand outweighs ability and individuals demonstrate 'I'm not coping' behaviours that correlate to ASC. These behaviours may have been held at bay during the individual's working life, but their working life is no longer available to them. The trigger to depression and other mental health issues (e.g. obsessive compulsive disorder (OCD); anti-social behaviour; sexual dysfunction and inappropriate behaviours) may, therefore, be retirement. The individual's working life that kept them on track and gave them structure for their day. This routine, being gone, no longer occupies the individual's life. Without appropriate support and intervention this population is at risk.

Being diagnosed with ASC in later years brings with it many concerns. When most typical people are looking forward to retirement, to time with family or time for travel, individuals with ASC may be dreading leaving the only life that is familiar to them plus having the added burden of knowing that they have a disability that was not known to them before.

When you grow up and live your life in a particular way, even if that life has difficulties, you find ways of dealing with these difficulties. But, for an individual diagnosed with ASC, suddenly those ways no longer apply. For example, they might have blamed others for any relationship breakdown they experienced. They might have become a workaholic to avoid social interaction that was too difficult to negotiate. They might have excused their lack of social prowess and told themselves that such social ventures were a waste of time, and so on. They now have a label that says none of the above was true; the problem was themselves all along. This causes severe trauma and upheaval that typical individuals will not have to battle with.

Then, if they want to access support and help for their social difficulties (those that accompany this new label which can no longer be ignored) they will need to share their diagnosis with relevant authorities. This means form-filling and the legitimate sharing of personal information with others. For me, just simple forms can lead to such anxiety that I get an upset stomach, can't think or function and feel really stupid.

Many high-functioning individuals will be faced with the kind of difficulties they have possibly spent a lifetime hiding from. For example, they will have to:

- seek help with administration (they no longer have an assistant, secretary, accountant and so on to help) of a domestic nature. This means they have to talk and liaise with people.

- take care of their own domestic duties (e.g. house cleaning, appointments). This will mean more talking and social interaction with people.

- own their age and possible health issues.

- face the idea of not being in charge of their failing faculties.

- answer the phone and the door.

- deal with unstructured and uninvited events that are not timetabled.

For others, filling in forms is the least of their worries as they face the reality that they are no longer as able as they believed themselves to be. In fact they suddenly realise they have a disorder, a condition, a problem, a fault; it was them all along and not the others they had blamed. This realisation can be catastrophic!

Transition

Decisions such as moving into aged care aren't always about the home we leave behind. Accommodation can work well for some ASC individuals who have intellectual disability and learning difficulties, for example, as long as it caters for the routines and daily structure they need. For others such as Freddie, whose story appears below, the idea of staying put in an aged facility is too difficult to imagine.

Case study: Trying to manage independently[1]

I'm 70 now and was diagnosed with Asperger's (high-functioning autism) when I was 67. I was given one printed sheet telling me about the National Autistic Society and how to contact them, which I did. I was not offered any assessment of my needs and the local authority and health service have never been in contact with me about my ASC, so I don't know whether I should get support to meet my needs. Maybe it depends on how one defines 'needs'. I get depressed and anxious and do not have anyone to talk to about it. I don't see a counsellor or psychologist but I'd welcome a chance to do so if it could be arranged.

I have some arthritis, some forgetfulness and a pervasive sense of an unfulfilled life and loneliness. The physical heart is fine but my mental heart isn't happy. I feel that having a useful activity, especially something with technological content, could help me with my present feeling of unfulfilled worthlessness.

This is pretty common in elderly folk generally but in my case it largely arises through my introspective nature. I never learned how to go out and find friends because I've always been too busy and too shy to allocate time to doing that.

A year after my diagnosis, when I raised the question of isolation and loneliness associated with Asperger's, my General Practitioner suggested I contact the nearest Aspie

1   Originally published in the National Autistic Society's newsletter November 2012. Reprinted here with permission.

group, which I've done. But it is 170 miles away...rather a long way to go. I don't think he understands my needs as a person with Asperger's at all.

I don't really have any friends, only occasional acquaintances, and if and when I meet them I feel I have to go along with their wishes rather than impose mine. There's no club or social meeting place locally where people know my name, so my only social relationships tend to be through social networking or forums. I'm interested in the idea of e-befriending and wondering if I could somehow participate, not necessarily to only receive befriending support from the NAS, but perhaps to give some online support as well.

I'd like to belong to a local group that's not only recreational but also doubles up as a kind of self-help counselling group, where members could speak freely to other members about their problems and worries. In other words, provide a kind of substitute for unaffordable counselling services. I think not having anyone to talk to forms the heart of the loneliness and isolation that many old folk tend to suffer. I haven't thought through the details of how such a group could be organised. There would need to be some arrangement in place to avoid get-togethers descending into prolonged agony sessions and keep a nice balance between social recreation and heart-to-heart substitute counselling.

I consider myself pretty healthy for my age. I cycle and always walk around town to do my shopping but I don't generally exercise for its own sake; there has to be a purpose to it. I like hill walking, photography, playing with satellite TV dishes, trying to solve my own and other people's computer problems, and generally messing around with electrical gadgets.

I live in my own short-term holiday accommodation but I travel a lot and am away more than at home. I have a wife in a far-away tropical country and I stay in her house quite a bit, especially in winter. Other family difficulties are so fraught I have isolated myself from them and drawn red danger zones around them. I had a family but I haven't been in touch for over 20 years.

I've been retired for the last 17 years, after taking voluntary redundancy, so I am financially independent. My career entailed living for quite longish periods in many different countries all around the world. Quite exotic, actually. I have a degree and was quite successful.

I had some difficulties at work but in those days nobody had heard of Asperger's – not even me. I was no good at multi-tasking and got confused in situations requiring compromise rather than perfection. I resisted attempts to promote me to positions where I would have had to manage staff. Although there was no support for my ASC-related difficulties, my different bosses tended to like my unusual style.

Looking back on it, I believe I subconsciously chose an unsettled, nomadic kind of life in preference to a conventional one in order to avoid all the social complications that living in a conventional community requires. In retirement the expat community keep in touch via an online email group.

I visit lots of places and I'm often on the move. In 2010 I spent three months in the USA and met some Aspies there. I met an acquaintance in Las Vegas and travelled with them to Mexico where I ended up looking after a country ranch. I've visited New Zealand several times and done quite extensive touring there. In 2011 I stayed with a British family on one of the offshore islands around UK and thoroughly enjoyed getting involved in day-to-day household chores with them. It was a very nice change for me. My career infected me with itchy feet to such an extent that I don't feel inclined to settle anywhere permanently. I can see that this is going to make life more difficult as I get older.

Within the constraints of what's possible, I suppose I do what I want every day. But basically, unless I'm travelling, mundane domestic activities occupy my whole time so social activities rarely get any attention. I want to do work on clearing up the daily tasks I always seem to have so that I can be free to embark on some bigger project in future, like joining a volunteer group.

I would consider moving into a care home if I could no longer cope on my own but I can't really imagine myself in that situation. I've spent my whole life being busy and wouldn't know how to relax. I'm well into my retirement already and I'm simply living it on a day-to-day drifting on basis. I can't think of any one person who understands my current unusual position sufficiently well to weigh up all my possible options and choices and make recommendations about what my final move and resting place should be.

I feel unfulfilled, as if I ought to be making amends for all the things I've missed out on in pursuit of my exotic life. I was taught and tasked by my grandmother to leave the world in a better state than it was when I first arrived and I don't really feel I've done enough yet to make that possible. Trouble is, I don't know how best to channel my abilities to achieve it.

Freddie's story is like so many others I hear, but Freddie's life is unique to Freddie. Having people who understand him, appreciate his skills and value his contribution to his community might go a long way to helping Freddie feel that he is achieving his goals. In his transition from work to retirement one gets a sense that he was let down. He still has some goals and dreams. These don't go away with age! Life is too short to hold onto regrets and unfulfilled dreams. It's even shorter as we get older! It's up to us and those supporting us to map the way to making those dreams become a reality.

Yet many older people with ASC are slow to appreciate what personal needs they may have. Having these painted for us, in a picture that we can identify with, is part of the process. Other parts include building awareness of why our need for aged care has come around. It is not automatically apparent to us that we might have mobility issues, self-care issues and other difficulties around self-care.

When supporting typical individuals one might use tact and the art of persuasion to convince an individual in need of care that they are ready to move to this stage of their lives. But in ASC, tact can go unnoticed! Most of us will cope better with clear instructions, clear support and lots of help.

For those of us older people with ASC who have always managed our own affairs, being told we will need more care in the future may not mean much to us. This is because words don't always connect us to reality. After all, we have been managing our entire life! It might be that we are easier to convince when we can actually have a say in such a huge change. For example, if a family member, friend or professional spends time with the older person with ASC then they can point out their observations of our daily difficulties. Because they are with us, it's easier for us to see things the way they do too.

When someone is in a wheelchair, uses hearing aids, has a seeing-eye dog and so on, we can see that they have a disability. But when an individual looks like anyone else, it is not so easy to appreciate that their behaviour may be a result of a brain configuration we call autism. This sentiment isn't just true for outsiders, though. It's also true for we ASC individuals ourselves. At times it's very difficult for us to 'see' our difficulties, let alone appreciate that we need help to face the various transitions we are going through.

As we naturally grow older with time, our individual experiences of ASC also change over time. Many of the difficulties we faced as younger people aren't experienced as we get older, while new difficulties come along often without us recognising them. For example, we may not recognise that we have physical limitations, need to wear glasses, need domestic support or need others to interpret our emotional or social requirements. Over time, patterns of coping have been established and we just expect everything to keep working as it has always done. Sometimes it is appropriate that others shine the light on these for us, sometimes we need help to discover this for ourselves. Either way, we need help to weather the transition.

Some issues rarely cross our minds as younger people because we are far too busy having fun and planning goals for the future. It is strange to wake up and realise that 'the future' is now the present.

Whether it's planning a career, a family, an education, retirement, or transitioning into an aged care facility, there are unique challenges for people with autism in their older years. ASC compounds the physical and mental problems of all ageing in general. So, older people with ASC will need different and varied types of support according to their individual needs. As we have seen, these needs will sometimes be quite unlike those of the NT population.

Therefore to ensure that growing older happens with safety, dignity and in the way an individual personally hopes for, transitions need planning. A number of measures should be considered, otherwise individuals will turn to other means of coping, which may include alcohol, drugs and self-harm.

Case study: My mum's lifestyle change

Mum is one of those individuals who escaped a diagnosis because she was good with figures and numbers. This enabled her to work in a bank. Eventually she ran her own business. After 28 years of marriage, the relationship broke down and ended in divorce. I believe some of the issues Mum has lived with are connected to her undiagnosed ASC. She has never had friends who understood or supported her. She is not good at coping with social demand. Alcohol became her way out.

Mum and Dad on their wedding day in 1940

Over the years her alcohol consumption affected her ability to think and process usual daily demands. During those years, when my children were growing up and Mum wasn't living with us, it became increasingly difficult to trust her. She would often turn up at our place already drunk. Not until Mum was in her late seventies, when so much damage had been done to family relationships and her own health, did Mum's drinking calm down. She decided to stop smoking and drink much less alcohol after experiencing heart problems. Mum realised she had to change her lifestyle or she would die. Sometimes, in ASC, it takes a huge event to emphasise that we need help. At other times, though, no matter how big the event, an individual may still fail to build a connection to what it all means.

Although alcohol and other drugs are easily available, most adults choose wisely when and how often to use these. But, for older ASC individuals the road to addiction is less easily resisted. Using alcohol and other addictive remedies to ease their emotional and social pain is more common among ASC individuals than in the general population.

According to alcoholrehab.com:

> …there are a number of ways in which autism and alcohol have been connected. It has been suggested that that there may be a link between a gene that increases the risk of autism and development of alcoholism. The research into this link is still in the early stages but it does seem that alcoholics are more likely to have this gene. It also appears that within autism families there is a higher incidence of alcoholism compared with the rest of the population.[2]

For older ASC individuals to choose wisely regarding events outside their control, they need to be aware of the options. If older ASC individuals don't access information typically then the information needs to be available in different

---

2   See www.alcoholrehab.com/drug-addiction/addiction-and-autism.

formats. Advertising boards in local community centres, local libraries, medical centres, shopping centres and all educational institutions are obvious places, but these are not the only places we can use. We can also use specific sites on the internet.[3]

Many ASC individuals are more comfortable exploring information online than on paper. Perhaps this is because so many of us (but not all) are visual learners, so placing the information in video format on short YouTube clips could be very helpful. However, even auditory and kinaesthetic learners benefit from video-formatted information because it suits all learning styles. The internet is also less confronting. It doesn't have face and body language to decode nor is it demanding of an instant response, as in a conversation. Rather, individuals can visit the information as often as they wish and take their time to digest it.

Summary

Moving on and needing further care considerations, such as being away from the family home and in a residential setting, will become reality for many. Every person with autism is an individual and one person's passion might be another person's poison. This chapter has shown what life might be like for an older individual living with autism in our current western world. Alcohol, drugs and other addictions are all too common in ASC. To tackle these we need to keep dreams

---

3   For example, see www.myagedcare.gov.au, www.ageuk.org. uk/?gclid=CPj8p8aNuMICFQYGvAodpZQAWw and www. autism.org.uk/living-with-autism/adults-with-autism-or-asperger-syndrome.aspx.

alive, promote a positive future that considers risk, finds ways to maintain motivation and builds self-esteem.

☞ Key points

- Transition is always difficult for older people with ASC because they have spent years of their lives establishing patterns to enable them to cope. Stripping these patterns away without providing genuine alternatives leaves them bereft and unequipped.

- To avoid using inappropriate means to cope with transitional difficulties, older people with ASC need support via appropriate information, targeted care, preparation for transition and adapted management according to where they are on the spectrum.

- Risk assessment is undertaken so we can organise suitable activities, not so we can avoid them.

- Alcohol and drug abuse are more common in adults and older people with ASC than in the typical population. We need to consider this fact when looking at transition in all its facets.

- Working with and supporting high-functioning older people with ASC is quite different from working with and supporting individuals with ASC who are lower functioning.

- Consideration of where an older person with ASC fits on the autism spectrum should inform our practice and aid our choice of communication materials.

CHAPTER 6

Preparing for the Later Years

Introduction

What kind of future is in store for older autistic people? The previous chapters show the difficulties that coping with change can bring; especially considering learning styles, personality and cognitive challenges. We have looked at issues of transition and building appropriate structures to facilitate this. This chapter offers ideas on how building a positive future is possible when people listen and commit to this growing population. In the long term, listening and then doing will save money, emotional investment, jobs and, ultimately, lives. Knowing the legal framework and being able to access knowledge about one's rights is a usual part of getting older. Supporters, carers and older people with ASC need to know their rights, and the financial and social supports available to assist older ASC individuals and possibly their ageing children, too.

Therefore, as well as speaking to those supporting older people with ASC, this chapter also speaks directly to the older ASC individuals themselves. It offers those approaching retirement brief yet specific information about the complexities of financial arrangements and the legalities of some family issues, and it explores ways of helping older people with ASC to protect themselves. To avoid loneliness and encourage autonomy, older ASC individuals need to be as prepared as they can be for later years. They also need to feel socially skilled and have a unique sense of self.

Over 60 and still working?
Plans for after work?

An autistic adult I spoke with, who is only 60 years old, and has been teaching primary school children for 30 years, was very clear that she is ready for retirement but feels ill-equipped and guilty at the thought. This is mostly because each day takes so much negotiation and she is left so tired that she has to go to bed by eight o'clock to cope with her job the next day. But she feels too young to retire, even though state school teachers in Australia are eligible for retirement at the age of 55. Also, this ASC woman can't afford to retire, yet the idea of having to stay in the workforce for another seven years is making her feel ill.

At the same time another ASC individual has a job that is their whole life and identity. They cannot imagine life as a retiree, saying, 'If I stop working I may as well stop living.'

Both of these situations are very worrying. Moving towards retirement age needs physical and mental preparation and planning. Even when you think you are ready, retirement can be an experience unlike any other. To move from full-time, part-time or even voluntary employment to being at home full-time is a very different experience from being home just to sleep, eat and entertain. Then, what about after retirement? What if I have adult disabled child(ren) depending on me? What if I still have elderly parents who need me? What if, what if, what if?

People will often say that when they retire they'll have more time for the garden, to read, to travel, to be with the family, and so on. To look forward to full-time retirement, retirees need to have and enjoy hobbies or be enthusiastic about taking up new ones. But what if your job takes over all of your attention and is your hobby as well? This is the situation for many autistic adults who retire from the workforce with very few hobbies or social connections and little information about what to expect next.

Autism support groups or agencies should be able to offer ideas and support for this season of life.[1] The transition can be supported by family and friends with information from an ASC-specific agency. Transitioning alone is generally too difficult to manage for unprepared older people with ASC.

Protecting those we love

I was sitting in the doctor's waiting room as my appointment time was close. I noticed two elderly people sitting opposite me; one appeared to be in their late seventies and the other in their late nineties. The doctor came into the waiting room and said, 'Hi Joan, please come in and bring Mum with you.' I thought how unusual to see two very elderly people, mother and daughter, together. These days many families don't live together or even close to one another. Independence is valued more than collaboration. Often it is assumed that older people with ASC (like neurotypical (NT) older people) will go into

---

1   The National Autistic Society (NAS) in the UK has specific information on ageing, and who to contact for advice, at www.autism.org.uk/maturity. In Australia a number of agencies are brought together on the website http://autismhelp.com.au. For up-to-date information in the USA visit www.autism-society.org.

care when they reach a certain age, rather than be a burden to their families. But this obviously isn't the case for everyone.

Being an older person with ASC can mean we find it difficult to adjust to the changes that come as our own adult children with ASC get older, too. As older people with ASC we are used to knowing what works for our offspring, and the services on offer might not consider their specific ASC needs. Change is overwhelming for older ASC individuals, especially those who have managed their affairs in the past. Some of us won't even notice difficulties arising. If we do, there is all that people stuff and paperwork to negotiate to locate and secure support for our adult children with special needs.

Wills and trusts

When we die, we not only leave behind all our worldly goods, we also leave behind our family and friends. After caring for a family member with ASC, one of the biggest concerns is around who will look after them when we are gone.

A will is the legal document that lets others know our wishes regarding our material possessions and financial assets (or debts) that we've spent our lives accumulating. Estate planning is the process of arranging for the transfer of these assets to chosen beneficiaries. It is an effective way of distributing wealth to those left behind.

It is important to seek professional advice as to what you would like to happen to your estate when you die. Each country has its own legal and taxation requirements. These requirements often vary from state to state.

We can organise for a special disability trust to be set up via a will or a deed; however, this type of trust only provides for the care and accommodation of a child/adult with a 'severe disability', as defined by the law.

A protective trust, also known as a special needs trust, can be established under a will. This type of trust is suitable for families with a child/adult who has not been assessed as having a severe disability. While a protective trust provides for the care and accommodation of the child/adult, it can also extend to providing financial support for their quality of life including recreation, holidays and travel expenses. Unlike a special disability trust, a protective trust can also support any adult children that the beneficiary may have.

Special disability trusts and protective trusts can operate concurrently for the benefit of a disabled adult child.

Elderly parents as dependants

It is not unusual to be middle-aged and helping to support your elderly parents. It is harder to be post-60 and still looking after your elderly parents. Being post-60 means having less energy for many of us but, if we are still involved with family duties, there is an increase in demand. You may be the one expected to understand and provide for your parent(s) but, as your own needs increase, the lack of emotional, physical and material accommodation from your parents may become very evident. Understanding this can help such older people with ASC to accept where their parents are at and appreciate they will need to find alternative ways to facilitate their parents' needs, as well as their own.

Superannuation

Superannuation can provide significant benefits to an intellectually disabled adult child. The trustee of a superannuation fund may pay death benefits as a lump sum or as a pension/annuity. A lump-sum death benefit can be used to fund a special disability trust and/or a protective trust as mentioned above. Generally, these types of payments are tax-free when received by the trusts. Alternatively, the death benefit may be paid directly to the adult child. If an adult child was financially dependent on the deceased, the death benefit payment will also be tax-free.

Generally, a deceased member's superannuation pension/ annuity must be cashed in by a child when they turn 25 years of age. However, this rule does not apply if the adult child is assessed as having a disability under superannuation law. The disabled adult child will receive the pension on the same terms as the deceased member for the rest of their life.

Choosing the right trustee

When considering these strategies, it is important to understand that these types of trusts need to be maintained for the lifetime of the adult child, so careful consideration needs to be given to the choice of trustee.

The trustee should be sympathetic and understanding towards the needs of the disabled adult child with ASC. They should establish and maintain long-term investment strategies and need to handle the ongoing requirements of the adult child as they arise. Selecting a professional, independent trustee company[2] gives the family certainty and peace of

2   For example, Australian Executor Trustees. In the UK, examples include www.holbornassets.com/financial-planning/estate-planning/uk-inheritance-tax.php, www.prycewarner.com/pg-wills-estate-planning-faqs-22.html and www.therightwill.co.uk. US examples include www.step.org and www.investopedia.com/articles/retirement/10/estate-planning-checklist.asp#axzz2IxPLsEw4.

mind that their adult child or grandchild will be well looked after financially for the rest of their life. An estate planning specialist can work with your other trusted advisers, such as your accountant and financial adviser, to implement the most appropriate estate planning strategy for you and your family's circumstances. Not everyone is in a position to leave their home and other financial benefits to family but there are a number of other ways that the right type of trust fund can help to support their adult children after the parents die.

Marie Hartwell-Walker

Dr Marie Hartwell-Walker (2007) has written on the subject of providing care for adult children with intellectual disability. Her words will often apply to those of us with adult children with ASC. As we each get older we are faced with the issue of what will happen to our adult children when we can no longer care for them. This section is used with permission from her work.

Marie points out some things you will need to do or think about:

- *Contact the local agency that oversees services for the intellectually disabled.* Often there are case managers who can help you learn what is possible. Different states and communities have different services and different residential options. You can't make choices unless you know what the choices are. Case managers also often are able to refer you to parent support groups, family therapists, or other professionals who can help you (and your child) understand and manage the challenges of this stage of life.

- *Don't just assume that siblings or other relatives will provide care.* Out of love and concern for their parents and sibling, it is not unusual for brothers and especially sisters to make promises they really can't keep. Promises based on guilt or protection of another's feelings usually backfire. Have a family meeting to talk honestly about what people realistically can and can't do. It may be disappointing to find that no family members can guarantee that they will take your child in. But it's better to know so that you can work together to find alternatives.

- *It is very, very expensive to replace you.* Maintaining and staffing a residential programme probably costs more than you think. Before you consider creating your own programme for your child, make sure that you have a realistic understanding of just how much money it will take and what is involved in managing it.

- *Don't assume that putting money in a trust or willing the house to your child will take care of the problem.* Estate laws vary from state to state. So do the rules and regulations for government benefits. (Sometimes having money or property in his or her name will mean that your child is ineligible.) It's not a good idea to go it alone. Work with an attorney and accountant to protect your child over the distant future.

- *Plan early.* Waiting lists for residential placement often are very long. Even if you think you won't need some kind of residential option for your child for another ten years, it is generally a good idea to make yourself known to your local service system so they can include your child in long-term planning.

- *Continue to work on increasing your adult child's independence to whatever extent is possible.* In this sense, an adult child with intellectual disabilities is no different from any other child who is getting ready to leave home. It may be easier, for example, to do his or her laundry. But if they are capable of learning how to do it on their own, they will develop more self-confidence and will be easier to place.

- *If your adult child's world is limited to the family, do what you can to help them get used to other people, including peers.* When people are comfortable around others, they are less upset when they must move to a new living situation. If you haven't already, find out if there is a Special Olympics programme, a Best Buddies group, or a local social club for people with intellectual disabilities and help your child get involved.

- *Plan for yourself.* Your child isn't the only one who will experience a drastic change when he or she leaves home. What will you do to fill the big hole left behind when your child leaves? Are there projects you've been putting off? Places you'd like to see? People you'd like to get to know? You may be rusty at being social or doing things you once enjoyed. There's no shame in asking for some support to help you venture back out into the world. Consider seeing a therapist if you find it hard to manage your feelings.

You've supported your child, cared for your child, advocated for your child, and loved your child into adulthood. You're probably exhausted. You may be scared. Taking the next step is a lot to think about. But worrying about the future won't help you or your child; embracing the challenge of planning for the future will.

Supporting older people with ASC

Specialist care

The likelihood of needing more specialist care will increase as we age. This may be compounded by the increased risk of developing allergies, asthma, heart disease, diabetes, needing a hearing aid or spectacles and so on. Unfortunately, though, so does the cost of provision for special diets and other health-related issues.

How do carers plan for these needs? Being aware of any possible issue and (a) expecting it, (b) planning for it and (c) being financially, emotionally and socially prepared will be helpful. It all starts with listening. Carers need to listen to be able to 'hear'. Once they have heard what health issues may be likely, these can be monitored for, catered for and appropriate strategies put into place.

Listening

Building comfort into communal living is a huge task in ASC. Being part of a group is not what we do best. It will be very difficult for ageing individuals with ASC to find their place in their own community without that community being attentive and hearing what they have to say. To hear, one must learn to listen. This is because listening needs to come before appropriate action can take place; listening means learning to notice and 'see' beyond behaviour and beyond taking things personally. Carers may misinterpret actions of older people with ASC by viewing them via their own 'window' of belief. In actuality an ASC individual's behaviour may be their attempt to communicate discomfort, pain or frustration. As such this behaviour shouldn't be taken personally.

ASC traits in elderly parents

It is also worth bearing in mind that many older ASC individuals will have ASC parents, though they may not have a formal diagnosis. At first glance these parents can seem invasive, over-bearing or totally removed from the rest of family life. Accepting that their elderly parents will often have ASC traits is a sound foundation that can help older ASC adults to respond to them appropriately. Acceptance lets relatives off the hook and enables ASC adults to understand that their parents' actions aren't personal, but rather are the result of living with their own undiagnosed, and therefore unsupported, ASC.

Belonging

We all need to belong. Even for ageing individuals with ASC who enjoy time and space to ourselves, having a place where we fit is paramount to feeling good about ourselves. This might not mean being part of a group or having to socialise outside of our comfort zone so much as it might mean having a group who accept that we prefer to be less social.

I love my family and my friends and I love knowing that they accept me for who I am. They know that when I am on my own I may be alone but I am not lonely. I know they are available to me. If I need to be with them I can let them know; and when I need them to go, I can tell them so. They won't be offended!

Health and wellbeing

With age, all sorts of health issues are going to come our way, both as typical ageing people and/or as individuals with ASC. But, because, as ageing ASC individuals, we are so single-minded, we might fail to notice events that we should be aware of (Frith 1991). Maybe our eyesight is failing us when it comes to reading the newspaper or labels on items at the supermarket. Maybe we aren't as agile as we once were and, without noticing, we tend to sit around watching more television or working at the computer. Maybe, because it's easier, we eat more take-away food and less home cooking.

All of these will have bearing upon our state of health and wellbeing, but we need a way to recognise them and to learn what to do about it. One way, as ageing individuals with ASC, that we can get the support we need is to give our friends permission to let us know if they think we are failing to notice something that is potentially a health issue. Another thing we can do is ask our local doctor to offer regular health-check appointments and have the medical practice set up a time with us. We can do the same thing with the podiatrist, the optometrist and the local physiotherapist. Having others support us in this area might save us a lot of anxiety down the track. Maybe we have old medicine in our medicine cabinet? We can collect it all together, place it into a shopping bag and take it to the pharmacist to see what we might be better off letting go of.

Day-to-day living: Diet and meals

If we are already in an aged care facility then menus and food are all taken care of. But if we are on our own in a unit or still living at our family home, but minus the family, we might need support with everyday needs such as meals. I like the microwave dinners available in the supermarket these days: they can be wholesome, nutritious and inexpensive, and are easy to heat up and can taste really good, too. Most supermarkets also sell ready-prepared salads and I like these as well. I have found many that accommodate special diets like mine, which is great!

Our circle of friends

Whether part of the typical population or one of those of us ageing with ASC, it is very clear just how important one's friends are to one's sense of happiness and wellbeing. Having others to relate to in our lives is crucial. We need people to talk to, share our concerns with, enjoy outings with, share special occasions with, share our joys with and simply be together or hang out with. The friends that are closest to me know me well and have shared in the ups and downs that life has brought my way. These friends are also ageing, just like me. This has many positive sides to it. We enjoy the same types of music, entertainment, shows, books and so on. We also appreciate our specific time of life because we are all in the same boat.

However, the downside to this is that life's end stage is closing in on us too. I am going to more funerals than ever and I'm saying goodbye to some good friends. I could never have imagined that my circle of friends would change so dramatically. For me, as an ageing individual with ASC, my friends are my life. When even one of them is missing it changes the whole dynamic of our social interaction. Friends have died unexpectedly and there was no time to prepare for this event. Other friends were sick for a long time and we all knew their death was imminent. Either way, though, once they have gone, life changes for ever.

This is such a big thing, yet very little time is given to prepare us for this stage in our lives. It's not that we want to dwell on the gloomy stuff, but it's important to understand that as ageing ASC individuals we form attachments and we base our lives around these. Should our friendship circle become smaller due to death of our friends and family, it's no wonder we become depressed and despondent. How can we trust someone else? What if they leave us too?

I feel very strongly for the people I'm attached to and love them deeply, and I can't imagine how my life can function without their support. Like so many ageing ASC individuals, I live in the now. With all of my daily life routine structured in particular ways I'm dependent upon others to take care of the things I need that I can't do myself. If they are not here or can no longer do these things, what will happen for me? This might seem selfish, and maybe it is, but it's a very important consideration and one we need to listen and attend to.

In practical terms these are very real issues and need to be talked about. Making alternative arrangements for those situations that might arise as we each age is very important. We shouldn't just expect that other family members (also ageing) will step in and help out. We need to formalise things so that we each know what will happen if…what will happen when…and what will happen as…

ASC choice and daily responsibility

It's expected that older individuals, especially those with good verbal skills, will be able to make choices and decisions, and speak up for themselves. However, this may not always be the case. I often hear such words as 'the choice is yours'; 'you choose'; 'it's up to you.' But what if you don't know how to make a choice or what if you do know but don't know how to tell someone? Then again, what if you try to tell someone but they are not listening, or their policy of 'risk factors' creates an environment that causes them to think that fulfilling your right to access certain things poses too many obstacles?

'You're not standard, you have to pay more.' This comment was said to me today, and the more I thought about it the more it felt unjust. If you need a gluten-free diet because you're a coeliac or if you need special shoes because you wear orthotics, you will pay two to three times more than someone who eats a regular diet and doesn't need special shoes.

The shoe shop

I saw the pair I wanted,
'Real leather uppers', it said.
I tried the shoes on, hip, hip, hooray,
They fitted my feet and made my day.
For two days I wore my shoes,
Then I discovered some very bad news.
The buckle, all neatly sewn,
Came off with a flip, whilst on my way home.
I took my poor shoes and my bad news
Back to the shop, where with I got,
Some more bad news and broken shoes,
For they would not replace them,
Either which way I lose.
They said they could fix them, for a price.
I said I paid already, not twice!
But the argument I chose,
Did not win the day.
They refused to assist me and sent me away.

Has this kind of thing ever happened to you? Have you felt guilty for a garment of clothing that dropped a button or the zipper stopped working? If we buy an item of clothing and have proof of purchase then we have a right to that item being in good order; and if it should break or be in need of repair within a short period of time, we have the right of replacement.

I've seen shops stating 'No refund or exchange' for example, but actually, the shop does not have the right to do this. It is our right as a customer to goods and services that are what they claim to be. If not, we have a right to challenge the sale and request a refund or the appropriate recourse or action, without it costing us again.[3]

As an ageing individual with ASC sometimes I think they see me coming! I just don't appear to know much about anything and I get taken for a ride. It may be a good idea to take an authoritative friend with us, if we need to complain about something.

Last year I was staying in a hotel where I had been told I could get a gluten-free breakfast. I spoke to the waiter in the restaurant and he checked with the chef to tell me which food I could safely eat. I ordered my breakfast accordingly. I was surprised when the breakfast came and the eggs were on toast, there was sausage too. I called the waiter again and was reassured that the whole meal was gluten-free. So, I ate and enjoyed my breakfast.

Unfortunately, within half an hour I was very unwell. On talking directly with the manager, who checked with the

---

3   Consumer rights. Australia: www.australia.gov.au/topics/ economy-money-and-tax/consumer-protection. UK: www.gov. uk/consumer-protection-rights. USA: www.usa.gov/topics/ consumer.shtml.

chef, I discovered that the meal had not been gluten-free and I was very cross. The manager apologised, and said it was a mistake and these things happen. I felt this wasn't good enough, but couldn't process the situation fast enough to know how to respond.

I shared what had happened with the agency who had booked me into the hotel and they were very angry with what had happened to me. The lady from the agency phoned the manager of the hotel and 'had words' with him. Within a short time the manager had refunded the cost of my breakfast and had also given me credit towards another stay at the hotel sometime in the future. Even if the likelihood of my staying at the hotel again was slim, I was impressed with the authority the agency representative showed. This quick processing and knowing how to respond in certain situations often eludes those of us ageing with ASC. All the more reason we need an advocate or a person we can trust who will speak on our behalf.

Keeping yourself safe

Knowing how to defend yourself if you should come under physical attack is very important. If you are not physically fit enough to learn self-defence there are still precautions you can take. For example, when walking it is a good idea to have your dog with you, if you have one; always have your keys in your hand (these can do damage if they come into contact with another's face, neck or groin). Walk tall and look straight at others rather than lowering your head as if you were afraid. Sometimes we must 'fake it to make it'. For many of us with ASC eye contact is very uncomfortable, but we can give the appearance of looking at someone, even if we just look at their eyebrows or mouth. This depicts confidence and makes the older person with ASC less of a target.

Sexuality and need for an 'other' as we age

For people with ASC it is not easy building relationships. Many relationships are born out of mutual interests and grow from shared working environments, shared interests and/or shared experience. Beyond friendships, finding positive ways to relate and build further social and romantic relationships can be challenging. This is especially true for ageing individuals with ASC because we can't easily access social forums where others might be because being social is exhausting.

To complicate matters, because the ASC brain is designed to work with a single focus it isn't so apt at dividing attention. This can be annoying, to say the least, for potential partners, even if we notice them enough to develop any sort of relationship at all! At the same time, an ASC person's single focus can mean that sexuality becomes obsessive and potentially problematic.

Relationships

Because typical individuals often engage in lots of different interests and are not so focused on one, they are better at identifying and taking care of their own needs. For example, if they need company they may visit their local pub, club, community centre or chat online, rather than feel in need of social contact but do nothing about it. NT individuals are also better at putting their own interests on hold while attending to the needs of others. This is an asset when it comes to social and romantic relationships.

Older persons with ASC may have a wide range of romantic and sexual needs but lack the skill to explore these appropriately. Many high-functioning older autistic people will have been involved romantically and/or sexually through their adult years. Some will have married and raised a family. However, many will be living with the loss of their lifetime companion and coming to terms with the human need for further intimacy with another human being. For others, intimacy may not be of a romantic or sexual nature so much as it will concern the mutuality of social contact, appropriate physical contact (such as a hug), knowing how to manage emotions or simply having an appropriate conversation.

For decades it has been wrongly accepted that older people with ASC are not interested in having friends, are not socially inclined and don't have sexual desire. This incorrect interpretation of an ASC's impact upon individuals has caused a great deal of damage. Of course, there are always exceptions to the rule; however, I believe that while there are those who are asexual, not interested in having friends socially, seem self-sufficient and so on, there are many more older people with ASC who desperately want to have a close companion and many who want a romantic relationship with that person.

Developing relationships with significant others is important because loneliness and feelings of isolation can quickly take over when one has moved away from home, family and other safe and familiar situations. Aged-care facility staff may do their best to offer fun activities but for ageing ASC individuals these times might be too socially demanding and so not accessible.

What alternatives are there?

Maybe we could organise more one-on-one occasions based around things that interest us? I do like to go out at times, but only with one or two good friends who know me well. If we go to the cinema, a pub, restaurant, or to the theatre, I know that I find it difficult to cope if there is too much noise or clutter. I need to wear earplugs at times to cope and I even need to make sure I don't get crowded out.

It can be useful to visit some of these places beforehand and prepare them to receive an older ASC individual. The world is so much more tolerant of children – we need to help the world become accustomed to those ageing with ASC, too.

If the places can appreciate that our nonconformist behaviour, and possible failure to respond to social cues and culturally accepted norms, is not a deliberate act of sabotage but a product of diff-ability, then venues, shops, parties, and so on might be more at ease with us. Otherwise, we older people with ASC can find ourselves prohibited from accessing certain buildings, facilities and services.

As we age, some older people with ASC may have additional problems around appearance, hygiene and grooming. This is often due to lack of attention to these details through failure to notice them. At other times it might be due to lack of motivation because of reduced energy. Some ageing ASC individuals who find showering very uncomfortable due to their hyper-sensory experience of water splashing painfully onto their body will resist this activity if they can. They may find it difficult to wear clean clothing due to not coping with the 'clean' smell or through the lack of familiarity of clean or new clothes. They may know intellectually that being clean and tidy will increase the odds of others wanting to befriend them, but their sensory displeasure, lack of confidence or/and motivation and possible lifetime of similar habits will not allow them to adapt their circumstances to accommodate friends.

Helping us adapt to our surroundings, our ageing and so on is one thing; but it would be even more helpful if the world around us were more accommodating, too.

Summary

To prepare for our future means taking care of financial, emotional and social needs. We need to make a legal will. We may need to set up a trust for our disabled offspring. We may need to accommodate emotionally the fact that our parents don't understand that we have needs too.

Many ageing individuals with ASC long for friends but don't know how to access or maintain friendships or intimate relationships. I think that the majority of ageing individuals with ASC would like friends because friendships are very important to us, but we also need time and support to know how to ascertain and communicate our needs. At times we get so overwhelmed that being with others is the last thing we can manage. Being on our own helps us to prepare for time with others. I need this time. I think most people with ASC need this time.

Just as for anyone else, our friendship and family circles will get smaller as we age. Knowing what this might mean for those of us with ASC and what we can do about it is essential if we want to avoid deep depression and anxiety.

As individuals with ASC, many of us will find it difficult to do our own shopping, handle our finances, organise a will or trust, visit relatives and friends, drive a car, take on volunteer employment, build new friendships and so on. Being on the autism spectrum leaves us with many challenges; but with the right information and appropriate support we can learn about and embrace these. We do not have to be left in a wilderness without signposts.

⚑ Key points

- It's not too late to prepare financially, emotionally and socially for later years.

- If you haven't made a will there's still time to do so.

- If you have an adult child who will need taking care of when you can't physically and mentally do this any more, there are agencies that can help.

- Listening rather than being distracted by 'behaviour' helps us to see the reason for the behaviour.

- Being an older person with ASC doesn't mean you won't need friends. It does mean you might need support finding them, though.

- Ageing means needing more specialist support (diet, exercise, possible aged care/domestic support). This support will need to consider your ASC and ageing in the presentation and delivery of meeting these needs.

- Loneliness is just as likely to occur in older people with ASC as in older NT people. But, unlike the older NT individuals, the older ASC individuals lack the skills and propensity to tackle this appropriately.

CHAPTER 7

ASC Dual Diagnosis, Mental Health and Other Issues

Introduction

Ageing individuals living with ASC have various potential health issues. These may include epilepsy, diabetes, coeliac disease and various allergies. Many have other comorbid issues, such as Down syndrome, attention deficit with (or without) hyperactivity disorder (ADD), depression and various personality disorders (Tony Attwood, personal communication; Wing 2000). Other ageing ASC individuals are blind or deaf or learning disabled. Living with dual diagnosis presents unique challenges.

This chapter explores some of the issues associated with ASC, dual diagnosis and ageing. It also explores ways to inform and empower many with ASC to understand and work with the changes they are going through, as this impacts upon their ASC and aspects of their dual diagnosis.

Dual diagnosis

Due to physical health issues, mental health issues and not having the social skills to navigate society's systems, older adults with ASC often do not access the services and support they need. However, there are many ways in which older adults with ASC who have a dual diagnosis will need to access the community. For example, they may need medications regularly monitored and adjusted and/or health and exercise programmes implemented. Of course, the ageing individual with ASC should, wherever possible, take an active role in what happens to/for and with them.

Case study: ASC and mental health

'Even though I'm taking the tablets, sometimes I don't feel normal. I have flashbacks of past events and hear voices at night. This is what I'm up against.' When Mike was a child, his problems were not recognised as autism. He was sent to a boarding school, where he was bullied, sometimes by staff, who were unaware that his problems could be connected with autism. Later on, his difficulties led to him being treated badly by workmates. Mike's father was a tailor, and tried to help him into the trade:

> 'I wasn't successful in the tailoring trade because I couldn't keep up with the others. I just took too long as a learner and was asked to leave. Afterwards I worked in a zip factory, on a machine. It was fine for a while. Then I worked in a handbag warehouse.
>
> Being a slow learner or, to a finer point, having a specific learning difference, I never knew what was expected of me.'

Eventually, Mike got a job as a trainee painter and decorator with the council. As ever, his inability to pick things up led to friction with his trainer. 'I did unintentionally wind him up. I don't know why. He was always saying, "You never learn, do you? You get worse every day." He was patronising me – talking down to me. I stood up to him once or twice and it wasn't very pleasant. I had to put up with that for about two or three years.'

Now 61, Mike recalls how his social skills let him down with girls. In the beginning, he was very frustrated, not knowing what to say. 'When I was 16, I was besotted with a young lady who lived near me. I had to write a letter – I didn't have the front to talk to her. That's the frustrating thing about it.'

What he has always wanted is a loving relationship but he has never managed to maintain a partnership. Enjoying the company of women has resulted in some scrapes over the years.

Nine years ago, Mike moved to a flat that he rents from his sister and brother-in-law. Being a sociable man, he has made many friends. They visit each other's homes and go to events, parks and exhibitions:

> 'As far as I'm concerned, my friendships enhance. I have friends who are understanding. I remember when I was overcome with emotion and one of them spoke to me and tried to put me at ease.'

Mike has mental health problems that he usually hides quite well. But he is deeply distressed by the voices that sometimes intrude into his thoughts. He is scared for himself. The voices don't tell him to do bad things, they just talk at intermittent intervals:

> 'I hear voices. Half the time I don't know what they're saying to me. Fortunately, this happens when I'm lying down. If it happens out in the community when I start talking to myself, then I believe that I could well end up being sectioned. You see these people – they hear the voices, and it's real. And I've been frightened myself, once or twice before. And it's not a very nice experience.'

Mike attends a day centre for Jewish people with mental health disabilities. Sometimes when he is happy, he gets somewhat exuberant:

> 'I know I get a bit silly. I can't help being somewhat loud, even before I was on the tablets. The members here talk about their lives, the past – get it off their chests.'

Apart from the activities, there is a psychologist at the day centre on hand to talk through problems. Mike is reticent to talk about the things that make him anxious and thinks that isn't really the way forward for anyone with mental health issues.

People don't always realise that his cheerfulness is a front and that, in private, Mike is struggling to deal with his depression. When he's feeling down, Mike finds comfort in music, which he loves. Sometimes he dances along at home.

Mike's story is one of so many. Being an ageing ASC individual doesn't exempt them from other mental health issues. Living with depression, paranoia and other mental health dispositions that cause discomfort and turmoil are more common in those with ASC than in the typical population. Some estimate the level of anxiety disorders to be around 18 per cent within the typical population and between 25 per cent and 84 per cent in people with ASC. The differences are dramatic but there have only been small studies with ASC individuals so it is hard to draw any real conclusions, except to say that anxiety in those with ASC, especially as they age, is much higher than in the typical population (e.g. Van Steensel, Bögels and Perrin 2011).

Mental health issues, so common for older ASC individuals, don't just go with having a dual diagnosis. Many of the older people living with ASC that I have spoken to said they had lived with depression at some point in their lives. Many mentioned that they had trouble distinguishing their voice from the voices of others and it was also difficult at times to know the difference between thoughts, ideas and accumulated wisdom on particular topics. This is an issue for those ageing with ASC because other people will take control over their life and tell them what they need to know and to do. If they have trouble separating their thoughts from the expressed words of others it will mean living with uncertainty and insecurity. It is useful for carers to help older people with ASC name the ideas, words and thoughts to differentiate which is which and who they belong to.

Stress support needs associated with dual diagnosis

Carers of an ASC individual with dual diagnosis need to distinguish the causes of the person's stress behaviour. An individual may lose their ability to speak, may flap hands and arms, may bite and/or hit out, may become frozen and unable to move (catatonic), may shout or rant, may be inclined to invade personal space or run far away, and so on. These behaviours are typical stress behaviours in ASC and, as such, indicate that the individual needs support, not chastising or condemning. However, if the individual is an older person with ASC, and the behaviour is related to an intellectual difficulty or to being auditory or visually impaired, this will impact how the support is delivered.

To afford the same levels of dignity, respect and agency to older individuals with ASC we need to appreciate that they experience life via their diff-ability, not like the typical population. We also need to understand that behavioural differences may be caused by dual diagnosis, not ASC alone. This doesn't have to be an impediment so much as a different way of living a fulfilling life based on the common dignity afforded to all human beings. If we don't acknowledge the impact of ASC and dual diagnosis upon the individual, specifically for them, we will miss a golden opportunity to build a relationship and an understanding of each other's worlds.

Case study: ASC and learning disability

I know one older person with ASC living with dual diagnosis who is capable in so many ways, taking charge of his daily needs, such as getting dressed, personal hygiene, feeding himself and doing his own shopping. He has a job that he will retire from soon, and manages his personal and leisure affairs. But his teeth are bad because even though dental appointments are made for him he often fails to go. This elderly gentleman has ASC and learning disability. He needs someone to drive him to these appointments and make sure he gets there.

Although he can make his own choices in many areas of his life, he has such difficulty with forward thinking that he can't imagine what the outcome will be if he fails to go to the dentist. He can tell you that his teeth hurt and he should go to a dentist, but this is a different concept from that of actually going there.

He has agreed to accept support to be taken, but we still have to build meaningful concepts for him through creating a story using his photo, and pictures of the dentist and the proposed driver collecting him to drive him to his appointment. In addition, the story needs to convey that he needs to wait at home for the driver to come, go with the driver to the appointment, get out of the car, go to the dentist's waiting room, wait to be called by the dentist, sit in the special dental chair and do what the dentist asks of him. After the dentist has finished he must again wait for the driver who will drive him home. If the driver needs to put petrol into the car this also needs to be in the story.

Some specific situations of dual diagnosis

The case study above demonstrates a way to give the older individual with ASC and intellectual disability some measure of control and a say in what happens to and for them. (Note that this particular dual diagnosis is often seen as 'only autism'.) Storytelling[1] is relevant to many situations for developing concepts in ageing ASC individuals with dual diagnosis. Stories work well for higher functioning ASC individuals as well as for individuals with an intellectual disability (lower functioning) if they are presented in formats that the individual relates to.

ASC and Down syndrome

Researchers have found that Down syndrome and autism spectrum conditions share many of the same neuroanatomical characteristics (Kent *et al.* 1999; Evans *et al.* 2006). In the past, for some, where Down syndrome has been the diagnosis, even when it is obvious that other issues are a result of behaviours not associated with Down syndrome, other possibilities for explaining what might be the reason for them have been ignored.

---

1   For more information see www.CarolGraySocialStories.com.

Down syndrome (DS) is a lifelong condition that causes delays in learning and development. It is the result of a chromosomal disposition and affects one individual in 700 to 800.[2] Although the two conditions (ASC and DS) are both biologically based, they are very different (Grandin 2012). Statistics about people living with both DS and ASC are scanty but it is believed that this occurs more commonly than previously thought (Howlin, Wing and Gould 1995; Schendel *et al.* 2009).

Individuals with DS are easily recognised from the general population. They have:

- distinguishable physical characteristics such as upward slanting eyes
- low muscle tone (as a baby, they may feel 'floppy')
- smaller stature and shorter fingers
- intellectual disability to varying degrees
- a higher-than-average incidence of heart and respiratory conditions.

People with Down syndrome may be easy-going or strong-willed. Some DS individuals like music, while others have no interest in it at all. Each DS individual resembles their family and is as unique as everyone else.

It seems obvious to say 'All individuals need appropriate health care', but we do need to understand how to go about putting this into practice for ageing ASC individuals with a dual diagnosis. For example, at times, stress support needs seen in ageing adults with a dual diagnosis may predispose families to unnecessary pressure. When medical professionals

---

2   See www.dsaq.org.au.

understand and can accommodate dual diagnosis, individual stress, for all concerned, can be reduced. This happens when families and individuals feel heard, acknowledged, and both diagnoses are catered for, not just the one. For example, catering for an elderly person with ASC but not considering their DS as well is only seeing half the picture.

SENSORY ISSUES IN ASC–DS

Being challenged with hypo- or hyper-sensory issues is common in ASC–DS. For some, any noisy equipment is overwhelmingly painful, yet for others it sparks acute interest. For some, having an individual lean over them or be nearby will cause great discomfort, while others can't get enough physical contact. Most will avoid eye contact.

LEARNING STYLE IN ASC–DS

Just like the rest of the population, people with ASC–DS are all different and will learn differently. Some will be visual learners and some will not. It is important to check with the family or referring professional for appropriate information on their learning style. Gaining an understanding of how someone learns and any sensory issues they live with is vital to the success of their interactions.

ASC and deafness

There is very little literature on living with ASC and being deaf. As we age it is more common for our hearing to become impaired, and combining information and knowledge concerning ASC and auditory impairment (hearing issues, not processing issues) is the first step to knowing what might be useful. Living with sensory issues will colour this knowledge; for example, the use of hearing aids can increase the likelihood of tinnitus, cause huge discomfort to the wearer and generally cause more issues than it aims to solve. Therefore, it is important to know if the ASC individual has sensory issues and to understand how they impact the person. Becoming deaf can be a gradual process so it is likely that the older person with ASC will fail to notice that they have a hearing problem.

Family and staff supporting older people with ASC will need to think carefully about how to broach this subject and organise a hearing test. Just like the elderly man and his dental visits in the case study above, carers can use the story format to help the ASC individual to know what to expect from a hearing test. The story could be written like a comic strip using the individual's photograph in places that relate to that person.

Preparing an individual for a hearing test may go something like:

> 'Jim, I'm wondering how well you are hearing the words we use, in conversations together, on the TV or radio, or any other place. I thought we could try something together to see if hearing is a problem for you. Would you like to explore this with me? If you stand with your back to me and keep your eyes closed, you could raise your hand when you hear my voice. Would you like to have a go? It's a bit like Sherlock Holmes. We are looking for clues! If you find it difficult to hear my voice it might mean your ears are finding it hard to hear words and they might need some help. This help could come from a professional audiologist assessing your hearing. I have some information on this for you to look at.'

Sometimes a story like this is enough. At other times it will need to be punctuated with pictures or symbols or both, depending upon the cognitive status of the older person involved.

ASC and visual impairment

Storytelling through pictures, photographs or print is not a workable communication format for older people with ASC living with low vision or blindness. Often, stories and information have been digitally transcribed onto an audio CD or placed into a Braille format to allow access for visually challenged individuals. People who have grown up with visual challenges and ASC may have been taught to use these. However, for someone who has developed low or no vision due to glaucoma, cataract or other developments, these modes of access will be new. Cataracts can be removed but vision that is impaired by another issue may not be so easily rectified. It can take some convincing for such older people to become interested in using methods of accessing information that they are not familiar with. The best way is to work with the most suitable method of information exchange but add an area in which the person is already interested. For example, use an audio instruction with a favourite voice or character they enjoy.

So, if the older person with ASC has low vision or becomes blind, and learning Braille is too daunting a project, there are other ways to convey and share information. The fear of attempting new things, such as Braille, may be due to their advanced age, over-stimulating senses (hyper-touch) or intellectual capacity. If this is the case, then using CDs, recorded messages and taped stories may be useful. If an older person with ASC is a lover of science fiction then using this topic subject matter can be a great way to build concepts. If they are gardeners or historians, using this subject matter works best. Capturing the person's interest provides direct access for family, staff and individuals alike, to gain access to understanding. (See also 'Plan implementation: Motivation' in Chapter 1.)

Communication: Assistive technology

Using software that gives appropriate access to information while at the same time enabling the individual to be more independent is a very useful means of communication.

Assistive technology is any product, system or service designed to enable independence for disabled and older people. It can be divided into three types:

- *Enabling* – compensates for functional decline.

- *Responsive* – alerts others that an event has occurred and so minimises the consequences.

- *Predictive* – enables interventions prior to the person reaching crisis point.

It is usual to find different generations of technology, generally referred to as:

- *First generation* – handsets and pendants or 'community alarms'.

- *Second generation* – home monitors.

- *Third generation* – mobile and wireless technology.

For individuals with a dual diagnosis there is also specific software that enables communication when words are not available, for example.[3] Software programs such as those

---

3   See, for example, www.ai-media.tv.

produced by www.spectronics.com.au (e.g. Inter_Comm, non-text-based email) provide the means for individuals, even those who might not read and write, to share with others what they think, feel and need. Such a program uses pictures and symbols (those with the software and the individual's own photographs, symbols and text if desired) to put together information that others can 'read', thus informing them of the person's wishes. Working alongside individuals and giving them a say in their own lives can only lead to a fuller, less frustrating future for everyone.

Misconceptions about behaviour in dual diagnosis

Many ageing individuals with ASC and dual diagnosis (especially those who are both intellectually disabled and ASC) exhibit 'difficult to understand behaviours'. When we consider the term 'autism spectrum conditions' or 'autism spectrum disorders', it is no wonder that those supporting ASC individuals attribute those difficult behaviours to autism or to living with 'disorder'. This term is misleading and leads to misconceptions. I suggest that if individuals hear this kind of terminology often enough then they learn to fulfil the expectations of others around them, and act disorderly. I believe the behaviour is more about a response to the challenges life bestows rather than the individual being disorderly. Another way to say this is: 'Could those challenging behaviours be due to the individual being very stressed?' Should we, therefore, swap the term 'difficult to understand behaviours' or 'challenging behaviours' for 'stress support needs'?

For example, when supporting an ASC individual who is pre-verbal and intellectually challenged and is 'creating a scene' because, for example, their lunch is late due to staff issues, it is not constructive to tell them to behave or go to their room. It is better to help them know what to expect if lunch is late. Preparation of this nature, placed into a story with appropriate content and presentation, might take ten minutes but could save hours of stress.

For older individuals with ASC, disappointment can be all-consuming and if it is not understood by their supporters the stress response can escalate. It is better to build into their daily routine an understanding that, for example: 'Sometimes meals are late. This is uncomfortable but it's OK. The meal will still arrive and there will be time to eat it.'

Auditory stories are particularly important for those who are visually challenged, and, likewise, visual stories for those with auditory impairment. When an individual is ASC, blind and deaf (and whatever else) the challenge is to develop communication techniques that support their learning in ways they need. Many illustrations have already been mentioned. Carers can use combinations of auditory and visual or tactile story material to convey information and set the scene. It is a vital tool to prevent stress.

Lack of motivation

Individuals may appear uninterested in learning the new technologies. This might be because they are personally connecting with what is happening for them but may not realise that others don't read their minds. Another disturbing reason could be that they might not have access. It's frightening to think that the lack of access to appropriate technology might be the only thing standing in the way of some older ASC individuals' capacity to communicate!

Being 'difficult'

Apparently, being old means being difficult! This is a stereotype that older people with ASC, particularly those with dual diagnosis, live with daily. Often life is more difficult for ageing ASC individuals with a dual diagnosis than it is for younger people. This is because being older can mean living with less support but with more expectations of them, because others expect older people to be more 'responsible'. I suspect that children and typical older people are given more leeway, because (a) children are let off due to being young, and (b) typical older people are better at explaining their viewpoint than older people with ASC, who are more gullible.

Older ASC individuals often have less family to support them and also fewer friendships than their NT peers. As well, many appropriate services lose their funding, so support tends to decrease as we grow older. However, if the older person with ASC is living with the type of dual diagnosis that qualifies as a condition for funding (e.g. intellectual disability, Down syndrome, hearing and/or severe visual impairment) then funding can be available on the premise that it is used for that condition rather than for ASC. This is relevant because ASC impacts upon an individual's life in quite dramatic ways. However, if an individual does not have a dual diagnosis and they are of typical intelligence, they may not be funded at all. Sometimes wise carers and support teams can use the funding given for the other, non-ASC, diagnosis for ASC individuals in a more general sense.

Independent living

Living with a sensory system that leads to being easily overwhelmed will pose many difficulties for those ageing with ASC. What if individual support needs are actually a response to the behaviour associated with the actions of those around them (such as noisy house mates, property going missing, appointments failing to materialise and so on)? What of sensory issues (sensory dysphoria) due to too much noise, visual stimuli, tactile and social demand and/ or general expectation afforded to independent living? See the table in Chapter 8, which identifies senses and potential sensory issues.

To take charge of one's life, one must be able to budget and manage time, relationships, family commitments and domestic duties. If individuals don't have close family to help them, they may need to ask extended family or good friends and neighbours to lend a hand. If they don't ask, others may not realise that the ASC individual needs them in this way. People are usually willing to help out once they know what is needed, but it might be best to not ask the same person to assist with *all* of the following: transport, personal hygiene, shopping, cooking, leisure, safety, appointments and relationships! Older people with ASC need help to work out *what* they need and *how* and *who* to ask for it.

I've written before about how people with ASC can build strong support systems and live better lives (Lawson 2003, 2005, 2006). Some strategies include pre-planning, making lists, having an agenda and reading widely. Accepting that there will be some trial and error is also useful to understand. Just because one thing doesn't work doesn't mean that with a little tweaking something similar will also fail. It is also important to be discerning about disclosure of individual needs as an ASC person. A good book to help with this is *Coming Out Asperger: Diagnosis, Disclosure and Self-Confidence* (2005) edited by Dinah Murray.

For individuals with ASC and dual diagnosis, finding their niche is a big part of ageing with dignity and self-respect. This also contributes to happiness.

Coping with medical visits

Ageing takes time, but it seems that in no time at all individuals are being plagued by reasons to visit the doctor, the hospital and other medical professions. At all of these places there is an understanding of what to do, say, be, and so on. However, older individuals with ASC may not know about or understand those expectations. When is it the right time to talk? Do I tell the receptionist my problems? How long do I wait if my appointment is for a certain time but that time has come and gone? What if I need treatment from another doctor or a specialist?

If I get told 'You are seeing the doctor' but they send me to a different doctor, what does this mean? Are they both 'the doctor'? Will the doctor speak to me in terms I understand or will they treat me like I'm stupid? Older people with ASC depend on professionals to be informed and to know how to share the information with them.

The individual needs to give the general practitioner time to get to know them, so should aim to visit the same GP each time. The carer should ask the receptionist to let the individual know how long they might need to wait. Ask if there is a waiting area where the individual can sit and not be disturbed by other people. If the waiting period is longer than a few minutes, maybe the individual can listen to their music through headphones? This way they may not be too distressed by the noises of children or other people in the waiting room. Maybe they could be given the option of waiting in the car and being called when it's time? Being an older person with ASC myself I see these accommodations of my autism and sensory issues as common decency.

When an ageing individual with ASC has to go into hospital, it is best for the carer to let the authorities know the individual is autistic and request a single room. This isn't always possible but at least people will understand if they put the curtains around their bed and don't interact socially. Hospital staff need to know that all procedures need to be explained to the individual, all staff should be introduced, the reason given for why they are seeing the person with ASC and what they might do to, with or for them.

ASC and mental health

Anxiety and depression are common in ASC, especially as individuals get older and are subject to greater change (Carpenter 2007). According to Tantam (2013), about one in 15 people with Asperger syndrome will experience depression. Mental health issues often begin in adolescence and may recur whenever individuals have to face another challenge that is new to them.

Lainhart and Folstein (1994) suggest three approaches in diagnosing depression in a person with autism, which can be used separately or consecutively, as appropriate:

1.   Investigate whether there is a deterioration in cognition, language, behaviour or activity. It is not common to recognise this as being connected to mood.

2.   Take an individual history to establish a baseline of patterns of activity and interests. Then patterns of subsequent behaviour can be compared with previous or known patterns of behaviour so differences can be outlined.

3.   Attempt a direct assessment of the individual's mental state. Sometimes this means talking to family and carers as well as to the individual themselves. Examples of behaviour that points to depression might include reports of crying, difficulties in separating from their parent/carer for an interview, increased/decreased activity, agitation or aggression. There may be evidence of new or increased self-injury or worsening autistic features, such as increased proportion of echolalia (word repetition) or the reappearance of hand-flapping.

Ageing with ASC brings its own challenges, but mental health is often not considered separately. Because anxiety and depression are more common in older people with ASC, these can get lumped all together as being part of the autistic disposition.

The National Autistic Society says:[4]

Depression of someone with high-functioning autism may take the same form as in people without the condition, although the content of the illness may be different. For example, the depression might show itself through an individual's particular preoccupations and obsessions and care must be taken to ensure that the depression is

---

4   See www.autism.org.uk/working-with/health/mental-health-and-asperger-syndrome.aspx.

not diagnosed as schizophrenia or some other psychotic disorder or just put down to autism.

So it may not be autism that is the problem. Assuming that daily routines and expectations are being explained and understood, these mental health issues (anxiety, depression, paranoia) should be treated as separate conditions from autism, but informed by knowledge of ASC and of the individual. Even though the research says that depression, for example, follows a similar course in ASC as in the typical population (Tantam and Prestwood 1999), it will show itself differently:

> Sometimes, as with typical seniors, medication is useful. But this needs careful consideration and should not be given out lightly. If medication is prescribed, just as for any other individual, it must be monitored. ASC seniors are more sensitive to medication. A dosage that suits a typical senior is likely to be too high for a senior with ASC. (Grandin 2006)

Grandin also brings the following perspective to dual diagnosis of ASC and mental illness:

> People with autism have very sensitive nervous systems. Some individuals may require much lower doses of medications than people with a normal nervous system. This will vary from individual to individual. If some individuals are given too high a dose of either an older tricyclic antidepressant or one of the newer medications, such as Prozac or Zoloft, there may be side effects. Antidepressants have a dosage window. Too little will not work and too much causes side effects. In ASC seniors, the first sign of too high a dose of an antidepressant is early morning awakening. This can usually be corrected by lowering the dose. If the excessive dosing continues,

the person will escalate into insomnia, irritability, agitation and aggression. To determine the correct dose, you must be a good observer. Enough must be given to be effective but too much can have almost the opposite effect. (Grandin 2015)

Due to the complications posed by dual diagnosis, blood and health checks need to be carried out regularly. Let's not forget, though, that exercise, social contact, healthy eating, maintaining interests and hobbies and experiencing autonomy all enhance good mental health.

Friendships are important to good mental health

Although I certainly understand the concept of 'friend' today, many ageing individuals with ASC and intellectual disability will not because they don't relate to the reality that people are separate to them. Many believe that if they have a thought then others will understand what they are thinking. In this scenario, obviously, other people must also know what the person with ASC needs. Teaching them that their thoughts are their own and other people have their own, separate thoughts is vital for ASC individuals' relationships.

Failure to meet our needs can result in our feeling angry, hurt and unimportant. Even now, as an adult, I still think that other people should know what is happening for me because I feel it, so they must too. Intellectually, however, I know that only I know what is going on in my head and heart. But because the feeling is so strong for me, I still need to frequently check out that the other person doesn't feel it too! Imagine the effect on friendships if you believe your friends are privy to information, such as that you are hungry, thirsty, unwell, excited or sad, but do nothing about it! Because we each operate on different planes of attention (e.g. Goldstein, Johnson and Minshew 2001) we can miss one another. Misconceptions, misconstrued concepts and misgivings are commonplace.

It is easy to see that an older person with ASC who has other health issues tends to find the whole arena of relationships rather complicated. Having said this, I'm told that even more typical individuals find relating to others difficult. Perhaps making and maintaining relationships is a bit of an art.

Feeling excluded

Being an older person with ASC means lots of change with regard to physical appearance, hormones and mood. This is happening for all ageing individuals, with or without ASC, but in ASC there won't be the same reasoning available, which limits access to understanding of what is going on. For example, as mentioned earlier, typical older people may be motivated to shower, change their clothes or be aware of presenting well to others, whereas older people with ASC may not notice they need a shower, a change of clothes or be aware of how they come across to others.

This is particularly seen in ASC women going through menopause and ASC men as they move into their late fifties and sixties. However, ASC women are better at masking their difficulties and may not let on that they are suffering. As younger individuals both men and women may have been motivated by family or friends to be more socially aware and take better care of themselves. If they were employed they may have been motivated by the expectations of colleagues or clients.

Once employment ceases, family influence fades and friends visit less often, the motivation can also subside. This may lead to other people misunderstanding the behaviour and withdrawing from spending time with the individual. This in turn can lead to feelings of isolation.

Feeling lonely

So, we realise that as ASC individuals age then often their friendship and family circles diminish. Finding others to relate to who are like-minded and enjoy the same things is a big part of the answer to not feeling alone. However, it is important to be choosy! Joining any old group because they invite you may cause more problems than it's worth. Criteria for choosing wisely include choosing a friend who:

- you are comfortable with
- wants to be with you
- you relate to because you have interests in common
- you feel safe with
- isn't bossy and doesn't want everything their way
- is happy to share
- you feel on an equal footing with.

Depression cycle

Older people with ASC quickly form rituals and routines. This happens for the typical elderly population, too, but they are often accommodated more easily. For example, no one disputes that older people generally need more structure and routine in their lives. However, if you are ASC, your objection to 'change' and your insistence upon 'sameness' goes way beyond the typical older person's need for routine and order in their life.

If one gets used to being depressed and yet not able to recognise what this is, why it is or what to do about it, then this becomes your norm. Sometimes the cycle occurs every month, every winter, every second Wednesday, always after eating apples or a particular visit from family and so on. At other times, though, the depression cycle is maintained due to habit, expectation, or the lack of appropriate assessment and intervention. *Older people with ASC need their behaviour monitored, evaluated and documented.* Privacy must always be respected and individuals must always be consulted and, as always, all interventions must be client-centred.

Building friendships

There is a saying, 'In order to have friends you must be willing to be friendly.' Friends don't usually just happen by. We need to actively engage in conversation and explore promising places where we might find others like ourselves. Places such as churches, old people's clubs, sports clubs and other clubs and associations might be useful. Some may feel more comfortable connecting to others online.[5]

Many older people with ASC are worried about the future. One of the best ways to combat this is for them to choose to play an active role in shaping the future rather than letting

---

5   Some websites that might be useful include
      www.facebook.com/AutismMomsSupportGroup,
      www.autismspectrum.org.au/adultsocialgroups,
      www.autismqld.com.au/page/121/Adult-Recreation-Group,
      www.theguardian.com/social-care-network/2013/aug/15/
      ageing-with-autism-know-more,
      www.autismeurope.org/files/files/ageing-report-en-sml.pdf and
      www.agingwithautism.org.

the future dictate to them. If individuals are too passive and don't take an active role in matters relevant to them, others will make choices on their behalf. They may make decisions that the older ASC individual doesn't like, need or want.

A note on mood swings and hot flushes

Trying to explain mood swings and hot flushes to an ageing ASC female is very difficult, especially if they also have an intellectual disability. However difficult it might be, it is important that they know what to expect, what to do when this happens and that this is part of being an older woman. As with all other difficulties in the lives of older people with ASC, supporting the woman with ASC going through menopause can be effectively done through stories that explain the symptoms and reassure them that they won't get hurt; that this is normal.

Case study: Maintaining mental health through studying

Good mental health can be maintained through hobbies, activities, studying, recreational interests and so on.

Being a late developer and returning to study as a mature-age student, I went to university in my forties. (I finally finished my studies when I was 57.) I needed lots of support from the disability liaison officer. I had extra time in exams for reading and writing and took all exams in my lounge room at home with an invigilator rather than in a large hall with lots of others. I needed time before class started to get myself organised. My support worker helped me check I had the right books for the right lessons, and anything else I needed.

The moral here: we're never too old to learn or to take up a new activity. If an individual wants to learn a new skill or study a foreign language, for example, their support team can help locate the right resources.

Managing sensory overwhelm, stress and anxiety

As an older person with ASC and learning difficulties I try to find ways to let others know what my needs are. Autism awareness cards can be useful tools when it comes to having to tell someone something but being too overwhelmed to speak. We can make lots of different cards for a variety of situations. It's a bit like having a shopping list with things written down so we don't forget. It's best if the cards are wallet-sized. The card can be taken out and shown to whomever I need to communicate with but can't do so verbally at the time – it does the talking for me. However, it is important to note that if an individual is totally overwhelmed they may not have the forethought or ability to take a communication card from their wallet or pocket and use it. It might be the support person working with this individual who has to initiate the exchange and request to see their card.

Example of an autism awareness card

When travelling or among lots of people, I use the Squease hoody and vest.[6] My Squease provides a buffer between me and the usual sensory overload that bugs me as it helps calm my anxiety levels. It works by air being pushed through fine tubing throughout the jacket. This causes me to feel 'squeased' by the pressure. I control when and how much pressure is in the jacket. It's like pumping up a bicycle tyre. It has a pump and a valve to let air in or out again. In warm weather I don't use the hoody, only the detachable inner vest.

At other times I take myself into my room to listen to music, watch a favourite programme or explore YouTube to watch special interest videos. All these are like 'tools' to help lower stress, build connection and facilitate good mental health.

These support strategies are also very useful in our communication with others. This is because they allow other

---

6   See www.squeasewear.com.

people to appreciate us more when we communicate in a calm manner because we are less stressed.

Wearing my Squease hoody and vest

Summary

Older people with ASC often have a dual diagnosis. Recognising each condition separately and then understanding how each affects the other is important for managing life and wellness.

Communicating health needs is essential for physical and mental health. For some this will mean using assistive technology, some will need family and friends to interpret for them, while some will write or talk to let others know their thoughts and needs. Being able to communicate and encouraged to do so is also vital for individual physical and mental health. Knowing how to develop good relationships and what to do to maintain these is an art that takes time and effort. Educating medical, social, legal and educational services is often left to families. However it is done, this is really important and needs to continue.

⚑ Key points

- Individual older people with ASC may have a dual diagnosis and both will impact upon communication.

- Sometimes ASC isn't the issue. Attend to each health issue in turn.

- Learning difficulties don't go away.

- Individuals learn strategies to cope.

- Sometimes individuals mask their difficulties. This occurs for women more than men.

- Technology can enable access to appropriate communication. When speech is absent or difficult to locate, particular software may take its place.

- Communication cards can also assist older people with ASC.

- Weighted items or squeeze clothing can create a feeling of calm amidst the stress of everyday living.

CHAPTER 8

Ageing Comfortably

Introduction

We all hope our ageing will be in comfort and in the company of good friends and family. However, as we get older we cannot guarantee that the people we relate to will be around to support us. We might have to find a community of other people who understand us, are happy to support us and will be around for us. So, the *first step* to ageing with ASC comfortably is to have the right people in our lives.

The *second step* to ageing in comfort is managing our environment, both internal and external. The external environment includes those things outside of us (including but not limited to people, buildings, furnishings, sounds, colours, smells) that impact the inside of us, such as our health, mood, senses and communication. The internal environment (our emotions, stress levels, and so on) impacts our sense of wellbeing, too. If we feel able, comfortable, interested, encouraged or unwell, unsupported, unappreciated and so on, our physical and mental wellbeing are influenced, which affects our behaviours and abilities.

The *third step* to ageing comfortably is having a sense of autonomy that allows older people with ASC to be creative and enjoy a 'spiritual connection' to who they are as individuals and to the world around them.

Maintaining motivation through interest

Maintaining motivation through interest is of primary importance in ASC, because outside of this individuals cannot connect.

When talking to older people with ASC about how they saw the future I had some interesting responses. Many said that if they had to move into aged care, they wanted to continue those activities that interested them. For example, Zaff suggested that if he needed support it would be in the areas that are important to him now:

> 'There are so many! For me the following are crucial: diet, health, being able to have animals, being able to have a garden, not being stuck inside all the time, having access to a pool, and being able to go on outings.'

He'd also want, nay need, to continue with the following to keep him healthy, grounded and interested in life:

> '…mostly alternative therapies, homeopathy, naturopathy, cranial-sacral therapy, yoga, meditation, breathing techniques. I use these on a daily basis.'

When I asked Sarah what areas she would like support in if she found herself in an aged-care facility, she answered:

> 'I would need someone to buy the wool for me so I could keep knitting. I'd also need to have internet access because being able to go online and check out the latest fashions is very important to me. And, I'd need to have access to a leisure centre. I love swimming, I can't imagine not being able to go swimming.'

I cannot over-emphasise how different individuals are from one another. Most individuals I spoke to had not planned for their later years, had not made a will and had not given any serious thought to what life might be like for them as they got older. Because ASC individuals find forward thinking very difficult, it is vital that they have informed 'others' who are willing to support them to live the kind of life they value.

My usual, please...

Being 'normal' for Zaff is being able to follow through with the natural therapies that support him. What if another person was in control of Zaff's day and what if Zaff wasn't in a position to communicate his needs?

Wherever possible, I encourage older people with ASC to document those activities that are usual for a fulfilled life, from their perspective. This list can be passed on from carer to carer, friend to friend, staff member to staff member. The older ASC person can be involved in devising, maintaining and, where necessary, altering this list. However, we need to make sure this information is kept safe and accessible. None of us knows when we might need to be in the care of others, and these people may not know us, our dislikes and likes. If they don't know these things, they will treat us according to what *they* hold dear and important.

Having a normal life means being able to do the things we like, that we are used to. Of course, this is different for everyone. What is normal for me might not be thought of as usual or normal for you. Imagine being told you could choose between a weekend retreat in the countryside or a weekend on the town. Which would appeal to you? Would it depend on how you felt at the time or would you know instantly which one you'd choose? If you would choose a quiet retreat but someone looking after you preferred time in town, the person might think you would like eating out, shopping and so on, because it's what they would do. How important, then, to make sure that others are aware of your likes and dislikes.

The typical population seems to assume that socialising is the norm. So much so that all manner of social get-togethers are arranged, whether it's a barbecue, a birthday party, a Christmas break-up or just time at the pub on a Friday night. It is very hard for typical individuals to appreciate that what they consider a natural part of life is more like a nightmare for many of those ageing with ASC. The exception would be if the event interests them or is an occasion they have practised for and have worked out a way to do it with least social demand. For example, they might arrive at the pub early before too many people are there so it's not crowded. They might have one or two drinks, sit at a quiet table away from noise and leave early, so no one has a chance to engage them in difficult conversation.

Within the world of ageing individuals with ASC there would certainly be many who are well practised at pretending to be 'normal'. This is especially true for females. Older people with ASC may have had many years to get this right, but once on their own again they need time to recover from the exhaustion of pretending to be someone other than who they really are. The need to blend in can be very strong, and many people give in to the social demand they perceive to be required of them.

The trouble is, the effort they need to put into pretending takes all their energy and leaves no reserves to draw on. This means that they need lots and lots of time to recover and can only take social activities in short bursts. No wonder so many older people with ASC need so much time to themselves. Even sitting at a table to share a meal with others can be exhausting!

Finding what it is that creates calm, value and a comforting space is important for all of us, but is vital for older people with ASC to enable them to cope with everyday demand. So often, we older ASC individuals need time on task (e.g. in the dining room; in the common-room; at a family function) and then a quiet space for recuperation. Typical older people also need time out, but not on such a scale as those of us with ASC.

Case study: My comforts

I'm the kind of person who loves being home. I can relax in my garden and enjoy my cats. But I also love travel. As much as I love my home, I'm a traveller at heart and roaming is in my nature. As I get older it's not so easy to manage my physical health away from home. I often use a walking stick and stairs are not so easy to navigate. It's a little depressing coming to terms with the reality that my life is changing. I need to adapt to the fact that I cannot be as mobile as I used to be. We all know this is a natural part of life but it still takes some getting accustomed to, perhaps more so as an ageing individual with ASC where it takes us just that little bit longer to cope with and accept the changes our body is going through.

I need familiarity around me. I use particular cutlery and crockery for my meals. Certain television programmes and reading material, such as *Bird Life* magazine, are part of my daily routine. My mobility scooter enables me to take drives along our ocean foreshore so I can go bird-watching when the weather permits. I cannot imagine not being able to do these things!

On my mobility scooter near the bay where I live in Australia, 2014

The effect of different living arrangements

For many, considering giving up independence and moving from home to a retirement village means having to let go of their family home. The home they may have raised a family in. The home they may have bought together with their mate who may no longer be alive. The home that is held together by a fortune of treasured memories. But they can no longer support themselves well enough to stay. In order to acquire the finances for the later stages of life, they now have to sell their home. This is true whether on the spectrum of autism or on the typical spectrum.

I've been shut down

I was in a room all on my own. I was in a room but not alone. For in my room, all on my own, I was enough to feel at home.

My comfort and relaxing mode were snatched away quite violently. It happened in a flash of time, I no longer was only mine. Your body, voice and smell as well, were forced upon me like a bell.

The noise was overwhelming, I no longer could abide.
The only way for me to cope, was to take my coat and in it hide.
Once for me inside its cover
I feel safe as inside I hover.
Waiting for that moment of time,
When by myself and alone I find,
My sense of: 'now I can relax.'
The overwhelm has left me.

But, how long will this feeling last?
How long till you return to blast,
This quietness to break.
I need to be on guard,
I mustn't take a break.

For in my most defenceless time
when I should least expect it.
Your voice will boom out again

and both my body and my brain
will have to hide and bide its time
till you once more remove yourself
and inside my room I close the door.

The new *DSM-5* (American Psychiatric Association 2013) identifies sensory dysphoria (difficulties) as the result of overload and/or under-load for many individuals with ASC. I'm pleased to see this listed – sensory issues are responsible for much of the discomfort ASC individuals live with. To age comfortably, therefore, these need to be noted and accommodated.

Some ageing ASC individuals have told me that their sensory issues have lessened with time. For many others, though, this isn't the case. Whether it's noise, light, movement, expectation, stamina, conversation, smells or one's own desire, these can all be overwhelming in their demand on ASC attention. This can be so much so that older people with ASC become immobilised and non-responsive.

The table below lists some the behaviours you might see in ASC if the senses are overwhelmed or under-connected. The behaviours are all common to those ageing with ASC. For some they become less bothersome over time; for others they are coping mechanisms and will stay with the individuals for as long as they are needed.

Location, functions and commonly observed behaviour issues of the sensory systems (sensory dysphoria)[1]

System	Location/function	Commonly observed behaviours
Auditory (hearing)	Inner ear; provides information about sounds in the environment	Noisemaking (e.g. banging on objects), vocalisations, covering ears
Gustatory (taste)	Chemical receptors in the tongue; provides information about different tastes	Licking things, ruminating
Olfactory (smell)	Chemical receptors in the nasal structure; provides information about types of smell	Smelling items, holding nose
Proprio-ception (body awareness)	Muscles and joints; provides information about where a certain body part is and how it is moving	Crashing into things and people, squeezing things and people, grinding teeth, biting self, chewing on things
Tactile (touch)	Skin; provides information about object and environmental qualities	Rubbing things, mouthing items, pinching/biting self

cont.

---

1   Taken from Mays, Beal-Alvarez and Jolivette (2011).

System	Location/function	Commonly observed behaviours
Vestibular (balance)	Inner ear; provides information about where the body is in space and whether or not the environment or the body is moving	Rocking, bouncing, spinning
Visual (sight)	Retina of the eye; helps define boundaries as we move through space and time	Covering eyes, closing eyes, looking at things out of the corner of eyes, flapping hands, filtering light (waving fingers in front of a light source), rapidly blinking eyes

Whatever environment an older person with ASC finds themselves in, the sensory qualities of that environment – the people, furnishings and activities – all impact them. These impacts fluctuate according to capacity and demand and will change constantly. No two individuals will be alike and no two days will be the same. But if the sensory profile of the individual concerned is established, the base data and usual behaviour can be used to assist that person to be comfortable. For example, some individuals will be fine in a common-room as long as they have their headphones to help block the noise and business of others.

Creativity

Sensory overwhelm can be greatly reduced when older people with ASC are doing what they love. Sometimes it can take years to figure out what an individual is good at or what creates calm for them. Some, like Zaff, thrive when outside, going for a swim or practising yoga.

For Mike, whom we met in Chapter 7, his connection to creativity comes from music:

> 'Music can be an excellent therapy. I find that the best time, when it makes me happy, is to use music as a way out of problems, it helps me cope. When I'm playing songs, I feel uplifted. Things like Sammy Davis's *Candy Man* and Frank Sinatra's *Pocket Full of Miracles* make me happy. I am hoping, in time, that things will get better for me and that the unpleasant flashbacks that I am having will be less of an occurrence as time goes on.'

Case study: The world through photographs

Elsa is 75 years old and still lives in the family home. She received her diagnosis of autism as an older adult but has lived all her life as an individual with intellectual disability. Elsa's sister is two years older, is not autistic or intellectually disabled, but has arthritis in both legs and takes care of Elsa, their home and their two cats. Elsa is pre-verbal and does not have access to speech. Instead she draws pictures for her sister, who uses these like words to construct understanding. Many of Elsa's pictures are on the doors and walls of their home. Elsa has drawn a picture of herself, which sits on the door to her bedroom.

One Christmas Elsa was given a digital camera and she is very happy to take pictures of the cats and other animals in the neighbourhood. Elsa is competent to download the photographs she takes and enjoys making books from the printed images. When I visited Elsa, the first thing she did was introduce me to her world through her photographs. One day, if these sisters need to move into an aged care facility, Elsa can take her photographs with her. These will help those supporting Elsa to understand her needs.

Emotional comfort

Preparing as an individual to be emotionally confident and happy is difficult for some persons who are ASC and ageing. Some individuals seem jolly and happy no matter what happens. The slightest thing can give them joy – a soft toy; listening to music; a favourite outing, DVD, meal or visitor. For others it's as if they notice every tiny thing that changes or impacts their daily lives. It might be a change in routine, staff, weather or how something tastes. For these individuals, especially if they feel the difference but aren't equipped to tell anyone, such discomforts can be overwhelming. So it is even more important that the people supporting these older ASC individuals get to know and understand them, and can advocate for them.

Ageing in comfort seems like an odd thing to suggest because older people's physical bodies are in decline, and comfortable might be the last thing they feel! As we each get older our bodies change in ways that we might not expect. For example, our toes and fingers may become slightly enlarged and our small joints may develop arthritis. Our necks seem to thicken and our shoulders hunch up. We may lose cartilage from our knee and back joints, which causes us to lose height so physical comfort may be hard to find.

However, there are resources to help. For example, using back supports while in the car, watching the television or sitting at the table to eat a meal. Putting one's feet up at every opportunity is great for maintaining circulation. Using heat packs (at just the right temperature and never beneath bed clothing) on your shoulders, back, neck or knees can be very soothing. It is important to maintain mobility by walking whenever possible. Keeping a certain level of fitness is so important. When we are older it's tempting to get others to do things for us – I know I have to talk myself into doing things myself and not always let these activities be taken over by well-meaning others.

Spirituality and values

One's spiritual life is not always about being religious. Meditation, thriving in nature, being free and able to enjoy a warm bath, a walk in the rain, a conversation or a story with a good friend are all 'spiritual' events in that they minister to our soul. This part of our lives is so often taken for granted and yet may not be appreciated until it's missed.

When we talk about ageing and ASC we think about the body of the individual. This is very important. But the individual's spirit and values should not be seen as separate from their body. Spirit and values are connected, and when one suffers so does the other.

Attending to the needs of our soul is vital for good mental health. This will mean attending to what gives life to an older person with ASC. It might be the joys of drawing, listening to music, dancing, watching television, exploring the internet, swimming, walking along a grassy park or sandy beach, engaging with natural therapies, yoga or meditation. Whatever the activity, the older ASC person needs these just as much as they need food, water and their walking cane.

We are one person. Our body, soul and mind are all connected. We need to be treated as a whole person. One part of us cannot be disconnected from the other without dire consequences.

Management plan

All plans for older people with ASC need to consider the comfort of the individual, though at times this will be really difficult. People are naturally drawn to certain others and choose to relate to them. These understandings need to inform staff rosters, domestic duties, family affairs, individual expectations and so on. Plans need to be made but, as always, these must be client-centred.

It's all too easy to judge a book by its cover, and this might be a mistake. It is so important to get to know the older person with ASC and keep good records of that person. We need to note what they like, what irks them and what they need in order to thrive. We also need to keep noting this in case it changes!

Summary

People are more comfortable when allowed to live 'whole' lives. This is very much the case for older people with ASC. Understanding the needs of an older ASC person's health and wellbeing includes understanding the sensory environment, one that allows for creativity and supports their particular spirituality or value system.

▷ **Key points**

- The first step towards ageing comfortably is to allow older people with ASC to thrive in a community that understands them, is happy to support them and will be around for them.

- The second step towards ageing in comfort is managing their environment, both internal and external.

- The third step towards ageing comfortably is having a sense of autonomy that allows older people with ASC to be creative and enjoy a 'spiritual or valued connection' to who they are and to the world around them.

- Being too social can actually undermine older ASC people's comfort. Older people with ASC need others in their lives in limited chunks of time. Their companions should listen and try not to do things just to suit the carer.

- The need for creativity continues into the later years. This might be the best time to study, explore, try new things and/or rekindle former interests!

- Maintaining motivation through interest is of primary importance in ASC. Without interest, older people with ASC will lack motivation.

Conclusion

As older people with ASC, we all come from different backgrounds, cultures, families and circumstances. Yet the one thing we have in common is that our autism impacts us differently. Some of us will have mental health issues to add to our battles. Others of us will have physical disabilities and need support from aides and equipment. Recently I was fortunate enough to have my single-storey home made accessible to accommodate a walker and wheelchair. My body is ageing but my mind is still full of endless ideas, hopes and dreams.

I've only scratched the surface of ageing with ASC in its various guises. But by focusing on the key differences for ageing ASC individuals compared with older NT individuals, I have highlighted areas where older people with ASC will experience their later years differently:

- *Memory.* When it comes to brain changes due to ageing, if you are an older person with ASC you actually have some advantages over older NT people. This is because your brain's elasticity will enable you to remember rather than forget; and it increases your likelihood of face recognition, which is usually difficult in younger years.

- *Movement.* Mobility issues can be similar in some respects for older people with ASC compared to older

NT people. But, in ASC we are more likely than our NT peers to battle catatonia and 'freezing' physically when under duress. We have a difficult time accessing language, especially when stressed, and our judgement of physical distances can be altered for similar reasons.

- *Sensory profiling.* Many older people with ASC live with sensory dysphoria and are easily over- or under-whelmed according to the demands of daily life. This is due to fluctuating capacity and is not so readily seen in our NT peers.

- *Language.* Being pre-verbal is much more common in older people with ASC compared with our NT peers and will mean that communication needs to be presented in differing formats to accommodate our differing learning styles. Even for those who do have access to language, sentences, conversation, appropriateness, propriety and interest will all factor in how smoothly (or not) communication is fostered.

- *Autonomy.* Some older people with ASC will find themselves remembering rather than forgetting, which may help with developing social awareness. But this will be tempered by possible increases in depression and anxiety due to changes in circumstances. It's important to build positive self-worth and autonomy to counteract poor mental health. Movement and mobility for older people with ASC is an area often overlooked. So often older people with ASC, unlike older NT people, are not equipped socially and will lack motivation to go outside, get involved with their world or tell others what it is they need.

Communication skills can be enhanced as we explore interests and assistive technology and ensure that we work with personality and learning styles. Sensory dysphoria is common in older people with ASC but we mustn't assume this to be the case for everyone. It is better to be keen observers and to note patterns of behaviour to help address individual issues around stress support needs, whatever the cause. Then there's language – be it verbal or body language. Each person needs the right tools to enable them to communicate effectively. Many people with ASC do this through stories. Telling stories is all about sharing information, building concepts and connecting. When individuals feel connected, heard and understood, they are more likely to live out their lives comfortably and in a way that works for them and for others.

Becoming an older person in the world of ASC is an accomplishment. It's just the beginning of a new chapter in life, not the end.

REFERENCES

American Psychiatric Association (2000) *Diagnostic and Statistical Manual of Mental Disorders* (Fourth edition). Washington, DC: APA.

American Psychiatric Association (2013) *Diagnostic and Statistical Manual of Mental Disorders* (Fifth edition). Arlington, VA: APA. Available at www.dsm.psychiatryonline. org, accessed on 18 February 2015.

ASPECT (2015) Autism Spectrum Australia. Available at https://www.autismspectrum. org.au/sites/default/files/Aspect%20Practice%20Ageing%20with%20ASD.pdf,, accessed on 25 February 2015.

Attwood, T. (2003) Keynote speech. World Autism Congress. Melbourne, Australia.

Attwood, T. (2008) *The Complete Guide to Asperger's Syndrome*. London: Jessica Kingsley Publishers.

Australian Bureau of Statistics (2014) *Prevalence of Autism in Australia, 2012 – 4428.0*. Available at www.abs.gov.au/ausstats/abs@.nsf/mf/4428.0, accessed on 19 February 2015.

Baron-Cohen, S. (2005) 'The Empathizing System: A Revision of the 1994 Model of the Mindreading System.' In B. Ellis and D. Bjorklund (eds) *Origins of the Social Mind*. New York: Guilford.

Belmonte, M.K. (2000) 'Abnormal attention in autism shown by steady-state visual evoked potentials.' *Autism 4*, 269–285.

Belmonte, M.K., Allen, G., Beckel-Mitchener, A., Boulanger, L.M., Carper, R.A., and Webb, S.J. (2004) 'Autism and abnormal development of brain connectivity.' *The Journal of Neuroscience 24*, 42, 9228–9231.

Boddaert, N., Belin, P., Chabane, N., Poline, J.B., Barthelemy, C., Mouren-Simeoni, M.C., *et al.* (2003) 'Perception of complex sounds: abnormal pattern of cortical activation in autism.' *American Journal of Psychiatry 160*, 11, 2057–2060.

Boyce, C.J., and Wood, A.M. (2011a) 'Personality and the marginal utility of income: personality interacts with increases in household income to determine life satisfaction.' *Journal of Economic Behavior and Organization 78*, 183–191.

Boyce, C.J., and Wood, A.M. (2011b) 'Personality prior to disability determines adaptation: agreeable individuals recover lost life satisfaction faster and more completely.' *Psychological Science 22*, 1397–1402.

Boyce, C.J., Wood, A.M., and Brown, G.D.A. (2010) 'The dark side of conscientiousness: Conscientious people experience greater drops in life satisfaction following unemployment.' *Journal of Research in Personality 44*, 535–539.

Brady, L.J. (2011) *Apps for Autism: An Essential Guide to Over 200 Effective Apps for Improving Communication, Behavior, Social Skills and More*. Arlington, TX: Future Horizons.

Brandwein, A.B., Foxe, J.F., Butler, J.S., Russo, N.F., Altschuler, T.S., Gomes, H., and Molholm, S. (2013) 'The development of multisensory integration in high-functioning autism: high-density electrical mapping and psychophysical measures reveal impairments in the processing of audiovisual inputs.' *Cerebral Cortex 23*, 6, 1329–1341. Available at www.cercor.oxfordjournals.org/content/23/6/1329. full?sid=3025e669-65d9-47aa-b184-a2be27458b51, accessed on 19 February 2015.

Brown, J., Aczel, B., Jimenez, L., Kaufman, S. B., and Grant, K.P. (2010) 'Intact implicit learning in autism spectrum conditions.' *Quarterly Journal of Experimental Psychology 63*, 1789–1812.

Brugha, T., *et al.* (2009) *Autism Spectrum Disorders in Adults Living in Households Throughout England: Report from the Adult Psychiatric Morbidity Survey, 2007.* Leeds: NHS Information Centre for Health and Social Care. Available at www.hscic.gov.uk/catalogue/PUB01131, accessed on 20 February 2015.

Brugha, T.S., McManus, S., Smith, J., Scott, F.J., et al. (2012) 'Validating two survey methods for identifying cases of autism spectrum disorder among adults in the community.' *Psychological Medicine 42*, 3, 647–656.

Carpenter, P. (2007) 'Mental illness in adults with autism spectrum disorders.' *Advances in Mental Health and Learning Disabilities 1*, 4, 3–9.

Casanova, M.F. (2007) 'The neuropathology of autism.' *Brain Pathology 17*, 422–433.

Casanova, M. (2011) University of Louisville, Kentucky, USA (personal communication).

Casanova, M.F., Buxhoeveden, D.P., and Brown, C. (2002) 'Clinical and macroscopic correlates of minicolumnar pathology in autism.' *Journal of Child Neurology 17*, 692–695.

Collignon, O., Charbonneau., G., Peters, F., Nassim, M., *et al.* (2013) 'Reduced multisensory facilitation in persons with autism.' *Cortex 49*, 6, 1704–1710. Available at www.sciencedirect.com, accessed on 20 February 2015.

Dawson, G., Rogers, S., Munson, J., Smith, M., *et al.* (2010) 'Randomized, controlled trial of an intervention for toddlers with autism: the Early Start Denver Model.' *Pediatrics 125*, 1, e17–23. doi:10.1542/peds.2009-0958.

Dawson, M., Soulières, I., Morton, A.G., and Mottron, L. (2007) 'The level and nature of autistic intelligence.' *Psychological Science 18*, 8, 657–662.

Dern, S. (2008) 'Autistic intelligence, autistic perception and autistic patterns of thought that we all share in different degrees – an update.' Abstract available at www.awares.org/conferences/show_paper. asp?section=000100010001&conference Code=000200100012&id=191, accessed on 25 February 2015.

Dickstein, D.P., Pescosolido, M.F., Reidy, B.L., Galvan, T., *et al.* (2013) 'Developmental meta-analysis of the functional neural correlates of autism spectrum disorders.' *Journal of the American Academy of Child and Adolescent Psychiatry 52*, 3, 279.

Dillon, H., Cameron, S., Glyde, H., Wilson, W., and Tomlin, D. (2012) 'An opinion on the assessment of people who may have an auditory processing disorder.' *Journal of the American Academy of Audiology 23*, 97–105.

Duffy, F., and Als, H. (2012) 'Stable pattern of EEG spectral coherences distinguishes children with autism from neuro-typical controls – a large case control study.' *BMC Medicine 10*, 64.

Ecker, C., Suckling, J., Deoni, S.C., Lombardo, M.V., *et al.* (2011) 'Brain anatomy and its relationship to behavior in adults with autism spectrum disorder: a multicenter magnetic resonance imaging study.' MRC AIMS Consortium. *Archives of General Psychiatry 69*, 2, 195–209. Available at www.ncbi.nlm.nih.gov/pubmed/22310506, accessed on 20 February 2015.

Evans, D.W., Canavera, K., Kleinpeter, F.L., Maccubbin, E., and Taga, K. (2006) 'The fears, phobias and anxieties of children with autism spectrum disorders and down syndrome: comparisons with developmentally and chronologically age matched children.' *Child Psychiatry and Human Development 36*, 1, 3–26.

Fombonne, E. (2003) 'Epidemiological surveys of autism and other pervasive developmental disorders: an update.' *Journal of Autism and Developmental Disorders 33*, 365–382.

Frith, U. (1991) *Autism and Asperger Syndrome.* London: Cambridge University Press.

Frith, U., and Happé, F. (1999) 'Theory of mind and self-consciousness: what is it like to be autistic?' *Mind and Language 14*, 1–22.

Geggel, L. (2014) *Early Tests Predict Intellect in Adults With Autism.* Simons Foundation Autism Research Initiative. Available at www.sfari.org/news-and-opinion/news/2014/early-tests-predict-intellect-in-adults-with-autism, accessed on 20 February 2015.

Goldstein, G., Johnson, C.R., and Minshew, N.J. (2001) 'Attentional processes in autism.' *Journal of Autism and Developmental Disorders 31*, 4, 433–440.

Gomot, M., and Wicker, B. (2012) 'A challenging, unpredictable world for people with autism spectrum disorder.' *International Journal of Psychophysiology 83*, 240–247.

Gomot, M., Belmonte, M.K., Bullmore, E.T., Bernard, F.A., and Baron-Cohen, S. (2008) 'Brain hyper-activity to auditory novel targets in children with high-functioning autism.' *Brain 131*, 9, 2479–2488.

Grandin, T. (2006) *Thinking in Pictures and Other Reports from My Life.* London: Vintage.

Grandin, T. (2015) *Evaluating the Effects of Medication on People With Autism.* Available at www.autismsupportnetwork.com/news/evaluating-effects-medication-autism-2292833#ixzz3PKmxh2CX, accessed on 24 February 2015.

Grandin, T. (ed.) (2012) *Different, Not Less.* Arlington, TX: Future Horizons.

Hahamy, A., Behrmann, M., and Malach, R. (2014) 'The idiosyncratic brain: distortion of spontaneous connectivity patterns in autism spectrum disorder.' *Nature Neuroscience 18*, 302–309.

Happé, F., and Frith, U. (2006) 'The weak coherence account: detail-focused cognitive style in autism spectrum disorders.' *Journal of Autism and Developmental Disorders 35*, 1, 5–25.

Harmon, K. (2010) 'Autism might slow brain's ability to integrate input from multiple senses.' *Scientific American, August 21*, 19.

Hartwell-Walker, M. (2007) 'Future planning for your intellectually disabled adult child.' Available at www.psychcentral.com/lib/2007/future-planning-for-your-intellectually-disabled-adult-child, accessed on 23 February 2015.

Hooker, K., and McAdams, D.P. (2003) 'Personality reconsidered: a new agenda for aging research.' *Journal of Gerontology: Psychological Sciences 58B*, 6, 296–304.

Howlin, P. (2013) Keynote speech: The Adult Years. Asia Pacific Autism Conference (APAC) Adelaide, Australia.

Howlin, P., Wing, L., and Gould, J. (1995) 'The recognition of autism in children with Down syndrome. *Developmental Medicine and Child Neurology 37*, 406–414.

James, K., Miller, L.J., Roseann, S., and Darci, N.M. (2011) 'Phenotypes within sensory modulation dysfunction.' *Comprehensive Psychiatry 52*, 6, 715–724.

Kalbe, E., Schlegel, M., Sack, A.T., Nowak, D. A., *et al.* (2010) 'Dissociating cognitive from affective theory of mind: a TMS study.' *Cortex 46*, 769–780.

Kana, R.K., Keller, T.A., Cherkassky, V.L., Minshew, N.J., and Just, M.A. (2006) 'Sentence comprehension in autism: thinking in pictures with decreased functional connectivity.' *Brain 129*, 2484–2493.

Kanner, L. (1943) 'Autistic disturbances of affective contact.' *Nervous Child 2*, 217–250.

Kent, L., Evans, J., Paul, M., and Sharp, M. (1999) 'Comorbidity of autistic spectrum disorders in children with Down syndrome.' *Developmental Medicine and Child Neurology 41*, 153–158.

Kleinhans, N.M., Richards, T., Sterling, L., Stegbauer, K.C., *et al.* (2008) 'Abnormal functional connectivity in autism spectrum disorders during face processing.' *Brain 131*, 4, 1000–1012.

Klin, A., Jones, W., Schultz, R., and Volkmar, F. (2003) 'The enactive mind, or from actions to cognition: lessons from autism.' *Philosophical Transactions of the Royal Society of London. Series B, Biological Sciences 358*, 345–360.

Lai, M.-C., Lombardo, M.V., Pasco, G., Ruigrok, A.N.V., *et al.* (2011) 'A behavioral comparison of male and female adults with high functioning autism spectrum conditions.' *PLoS One 6*, 6, e20835.

Lainhart, J.E., and Folstein, S.E. (1994) 'Affective Disorders in people with autism: areview of published cases.' *Journal of Autism and Developmental Disorders 24*, 587–601.

Lawson, W. (1998/2000) *Life Behind Glass.* London: Jessica Kingsley Publishers.

Lawson, W. (2003) *Build Your Own Life.* London: Jessica Kingsley Publishers.

Lawson, W. (2005) *Sex, Sexuality and the Autism Spectrum.* London: Jessica Kingsley Publishers.

Lawson, W. (2006) *Friendships: The Aspie Way.* London: Jessica Kingsley Publishers.

Lawson, W. (2011) *The Passionate Mind: How Individuals with Autism Learn.* London: Jessica Kingsley Publishers.

Lawson, W. (2013) 'Sensory connection, interest/attention and gamma synchrony in autism, brain connections and preoccupation.' *Medical Hypotheses 80*, 3, 284–288.

Mayer, J.L., and Heaton, P.F. (2014) 'Age and sensory processing abnormalities predict declines in encoding and recall of temporally manipulated speech in high-functioning adults with ASD.' *Journal of the International Society Autism Research 7*, 1, 40–49.

Mays, N.M., Beal-Alvarez, J., and Jolivette, K. (2011) 'Using movement-based sensory interventions to address self-stimulatory behaviors in students with autism.' *Teaching Exceptional Children 43*, 6, 46–52.

Mukaetova-Ladinska, E., Perry, E., Baron, M., and Povey, C. (2011) 'Ageing in people with autistic spectrum disorder.' *International Journal of Geriatric Psychiatry 27*, 109–118.

Murray, D. (ed.) (2005) *Coming out Asperger: Diagnosis, Disclosure and Self-Confidence.* London: Jessica Kingsley Publishers.

Murray, D.K.C. (1992) 'Attention Tunneling and Autism.' In P. Shattock and G. Linfoot (eds) *Living with Autism: The Individual, the Family and the Professional.* Sunderland: Autism Research Unit, University of Sunderland.

Murray, D.K.C., Lesser, M., and Lawson, W. (2005) 'Attention, monotropism and the diagnostic criteria for autism.' *Autism 9,* 2, 139–156.

National Autistic Society (NAS) (2013) *Getting On? Growing Older with Autism. A Report for Campaigners.* London: National Autistic Society.

Oberman, L.M., and Pascual-Leone, A. (2014) 'Hyperplasticity in autism spectrum disorder confers protection from Alzheimer's disease.' *Medical. Hypotheses 83,* 3, 337–342.

Pai, M., and Carr, D. (2010) 'Do personality traits moderate the effect of late-life spousal loss on psychological distress?' *Journal of Health and Social Behavior 51,* 183–199.

Scheeren, A.M., Koot, H.M., and Begeer, S. (2012) 'Social interaction style of children and adolescents with high-functioning autism spectrum disorder.' *Journal of Autism and Developmental Disorders 42,* 10, 2046–2055.

Schendel, D.E., Autry, A., Wines, R. and Moore C. (2009) 'The co-occurrence of autism and birth defects: prevalence and risk in a population-based cohort.' *Developmental Medicine and Child Neurology 51,* 10, 779–786.

Sokhadze, E.M., Baruth, J.M., Sears, L., Sokhadze, G.E., *et al.* (2012) 'Event-related potential study of attention regulation during illusory figure categorization task in ADHD, autism spectrum disorder, and typical children.' *Journal of Neurotherapy: Investigations in Neuromodulation, Neurofeedback and Applied Neuroscience 16,* 1, 12–31.

Schneider, W. (2011) Personal information. Available at www.lrdc.pitt.edu/schneiderlab/content/60-minutes-20120716.asp, accessed on 24 February 2015.

Tantam, D. (2013) *Autism Spectrum Disorders: Through the Life Span.* London: Jessica Kingsley Publishers.

Tantam, D., and Prestwood, S. (1999) *A Mind of One's Own: A Guide to the Special Difficulties and Needs of the More Able Person with Autism or Asperger Syndrome* (3rd edition). London: National Autistic Society.

Tonge, B.J., Dissanayake, C., and Brereton, A.V. (1994) 'Autism: 50 years on from Kanner.' *Journal of Pediatric Child Health 30,* 2, 102–107.

van Steensel, F.J.A., Bögels, S.M., and Perrin, S. (2011) 'Anxiety disorders in children and adolescents with Autistic Spectrum Disorders: a meta-analysis.' *Clinical Child and Family Psychology Review 14,* 3, 302–317.

Wing, L. (2000) 'Past and Future Research on Asperger Syndrome.' In A. Klin, F. Volkmar and S. Sparrow (eds) *Asperger Syndrome.* New York: Guilford Press.

Wodka, E.L., Mathy, P., and Kalb, L. (2013) 'Predictors of phrase and fluent speech in children with autism and severe language delay.' *Paediatrics 131,* 4, e1128–e1134.

Worley, J.A., and Matson, J.L. (2011) 'Psychiatric symptoms in children diagnosed with an Autism Spectrum Disorder: an examination of gender differences.' *Research in Autism Spectrum Disorders 5,* 3, 1086–1091.

Wylie, P., Lawson, W., and Beardon, L. (2015) *Nine Degrees of Autism.* London: Routledge.

INDEX

Sub-headings in *italics* indicate tables and figures.